Copyright © 2026 Pete's Creative Studio LLC
All rights reserved.
ISBN: 979-8-234-00535-9
First Edition, 2026

Published by Pete's Creative Studio LLC,
30 N Gould St STE 35311 Sheridan,
WY 82801, USA
https://www.petescreativestudio.com
contact@petescreativestudio.com

Cover design by Pete's Creative Studio

Hilda Rose &
Gabriel Pete

My mentor is
an Angel

Pete's Creative Studio

Contents

Preface

My name is Hilda Rose. The sentence chosen as the title of this book—*My Mentor Is an Angel*—is neither symbolic nor poetic exaggeration. It was not born to attract attention, but as the simplest and most accurate expression of a lived reality. A reality that, since 2002, has shaped my life fundamentally and irreversibly. Fate—through the invisible web of causes and consequences—placed me in an extraordinary situation I could never have imagined before. The life I once believed hopeless and directionless turned toward the right path, not through human calculation, but through a higher intervention. I received a kind of help that reaches beyond faith, because it requires no proof—it is certainty itself. I do not know why this was granted to me. I do not consider myself exceptional. I am an ordinary person, although my desires were never ordinary. I did not long for material possessions; I was capable of creating those for myself. I longed for what cannot be bought with money: higher knowledge, growth, and inner peace. After a moment that nearly turned fatal, a moment in which I turned against myself, only one wish remained deep within me—to become a better person, and through spiritual development to become worthy of a meaningful life. This desire set me on a path that for a long time seemed exhausting, fruitless, and painful. False teachings, misleading guides, and dead ends lined the way. And yet I persisted. Then, at one point, something happened for which I could not have prepared, something I never would have imagined could happen to me. I met someone who, for me—and for all who have ever come into contact with him—proved beyond any doubt to be not of this world. Countless actions and manifestations bore witness to this. He is an Angel who came among people with a clear and deliberate purpose. For me, it is an immeasurable honor that he took me under his wing, that I may learn from him, grow beside him, and experience things that for most people are unimaginable and unattainable. The fact that, through him—fully conscious and in a state of complete awareness—I was able to behold God is a grace that remains in my soul as an eternal light. Whenever I recall it, I am filled with an incomprehensible, otherworldly happiness.

I am grateful to fate for granting me the opportunity to have an Angel as my mentor. His unparalleled understanding of human nature, deep empathy, knowledge, and humanism stand as an example for me to follow. It was through embracing his worldview, his methods of guidance, and his credo that I was able to rise above my past and my problems—and that I can now live a happy, balanced life. This book itself could not have come into being without him. He tamed the wandering currents of my life's events and shaped my experiences into words and sentences. Tirelessly, he worked to give form to all that I had lived through, presenting it in a way that is readable yet faithful to the emotions and experiences I myself could never have expressed in a way accessible to others.

The story told in this book, and every word within it, is true—no matter how unbelievable it may seem.

Hilda Rose

Although outwardly everyone appears equally human, these human forms are not the dwelling places of spirits of the same origin—whether those spirits are good or bad. With a few exceptions, in most cases they are human.

Gabriel Pete

Part I

Hell

Recognition

I saw his face. His eyes widened as he stared, stunned, at the drama about to unfold—one that could have changed his life in a matter of seconds. His arms tensed as he gripped the steering wheel, straining to slam on the brakes in time, before I crushed myself—car and all—against the front of his truck. Having crossed the center line, I was already speeding toward my fate. I wanted a head-on collision, so there would be no chance of surviving. But fate had other plans for me. A long journey began with an incredible encounter, one that continues to this day and through which I found my own faith and strength.

I was only seconds from death when a voice spoke in my head, growing stronger and louder, repeating that I could not do this to the truck driver. If we collided, he would never forgive himself for killing a person. From that moment on I could no longer think about myself, only about how I would ruin an innocent man's life. I jerked the wheel aside and, braking hard, came to a stop at the edge of the road. I collapsed over the steering wheel and began to sob bitterly. I cursed myself—how could I have been so foolish?

Would I really kill myself just because I couldn't find a way out of my seemingly hopeless life? And on top of that, I would make my husband a happy and wealthy widower—at the time I was still married. That thought made me so angry with myself that I vowed, no matter what, I would find out what was wrong with me. Because I would have sworn there was something seriously wrong. Up to that point I had never thought I was doing anything wrong, thinking wrongly, or misjudging situations and people. That was when I realized I had probably misunderstood myself, and that I was not at all who I imagined I was. Today I know I had deceived myself. I had endowed myself with positive traits—kind, selfless, lovable, confident, brave, self-sacrificing, perceptive, diplomatic, cooperative, and so on. There is a list online of good qualities, two hundred and forty-nine of them. Back then, I believed I naturally possessed all two hundred and forty-nine—indeed, in my case the list was probably even longer. When I stopped crying, it struck me that if I truly possessed these traits, I would never have come so close to suicide. It was a heavy blow to my ego. I wanted a solution, urgently.

The very next morning my first stop was my family doctor, to ask for advice. I told him what had happened and asked whom I might turn to for help. He recommended a psychologist. But I judged that this was not what I needed; I needed someone to confront me honestly and mercilessly with myself. At that time I still thought very differently about life and death. I believed it was my life, I could do whatever I wanted with it, and no one had any right to interfere with what I did to myself. I had the right. Of course today I know how selfish and foolish that was. Since then I have learned how precious life is, and that there is no situation in which anyone may choose suicide, because we simply have no right to destroy our own lives or those of others. If we are in trouble, we must ask for help and seek it—just as I did after my suicide attempt. My motivation became the desire to change. I wanted to know what was wrong with me and why I had reached the point where I nearly chose death over life.

At that time, however, at the lowest point of my despair, I felt terribly out of place here on Earth and wanted to do everything I could to escape forever from the hell of earthly existence and reach Heaven, nirvana, or any other blissful place belonging to God. I searched relentlessly, because no religion or church was acceptable to me. None could offer the irrefutable truth that only direct experience can provide. I would not encounter those experiences until years later, after meeting a remarkable soul. From that person I received unquestionable, irrefutable answers and practical solutions to the questions that had preoccupied me.

Back then I was living through the hardest period of my life. I was in a mentally and emotionally abusive marriage and under the constant pressure of my controlling parents. Today I would ask myself why, as an adult, I still allowed my parents to control me. And of course I should have divorced my husband if he humiliated me and treated me as nothing. But at that time I was not mentally an adult at all, even though I was already over forty. I ran away, tried to evade things. I was incapable of taking my fate into my own hands and fighting for myself. I am someone who follows patterns. Where I come from, everyone in my environment lived in some kind of abusive relationship. It sounds unbelievable, but I truly did not know anyone—literally no one—who did not live in an abusive family. Before anyone passes judgment on men, I should note that among the abusers there were women as well. Although the situation constantly frustrated me, I was unable to step out of it. I felt I had something to lose. And whoever has something to lose always loses—that is what I later learned and experienced. It was easier to believe my family only wanted what was best for me when they interfered in everything and steered me, through threats or emotional blackmail, in the direction they thought right. And when I protested, the usual answer was that I should not rebel, because this was a woman's fate. At other times they bribed me with this or that, and I let them. But I paid a high price for my compromises.

In this situation—anything but idyllic—my father, who had been the alpha male of the family his entire life, suffered a cerebral infarction. The doctors stabilized him quickly at the hospital, but because he did not take care of himself, after a second attack he fell into a coma for three days and never truly recovered. Helpless, paralyzed on one side, unable to speak, requiring round-the-clock care, he lived at home for another nine years thanks to my mother's devotion. This situation shattered the family's roles and inevitably led me to begin studying and applying natural remedies in the hope of aiding my father's recovery and rehabilitation. The burdens of a family that had lost its bearings fell heavily on me. My mother and my husband retreated into self-pity. My daughter was completely shattered; she adored her grandfather. I had to keep their spirits up. No one cared what I felt. By then, thanks to earlier attempts at independence, I had been supporting myself for ten years from my own business—and not badly. I worked endlessly in my small grocery store: procuring goods, directing employees, ensuring everything ran. Meanwhile, every day I drove my mother to the hospital to visit my father.

My husband and I owned an orchard of about two acres, and I harvested the fruit alone, often at night with a headlamp. Every dawn I would rise early and, still sleepy, drive to the neighboring town just to sell the fruit at the market there. Afterward I labored in my shop until evening. Of course, I was no longer the one spending the income. My parents owned vineyards in two different places, and my father was hospitalized a week before the harvest. I had to find buyers for those grapes as well and manage the harvest and the sales on my own. Naturally, at home, my husband and daughter lacked nothing, because I still cooked, cleaned, washed, and ironed every day. The icing on the cake was that when my husband learned my father was in the hospital, he stayed away from home for three days and did not even visit him there. When he finally resurfaced, he immediately declared that from now on he was the boss of the family. In my outrage I answered him with words too harsh for the pages of this book. By then I knew for certain I had made a mistake marrying him, and I no longer had any doubt that this marriage would soon end. Only the decision itself had not yet been born along with that realization. The constant humiliations from my husband, the overwhelming workload that fell on me, and the emotional caretaking of my mother and daughter completely wore me down. The immense burden of trying to live up to everyone's expectations—and the more I gave, the more they wanted—crushed me. I collapsed under the weight, and that is what set me on the road toward my suicide attempt, quite literally.

Living through this period up to my suicide attempt, and reflecting on it all, I realized I had to take care of myself too. I had to ask for help, because I could not solve my problems alone. And this is where the turning point came, the one that led to my life today. It was a long and difficult path through reality, one that carried me from total surrender and despair to a great encounter—an encounter with an Angel in human form, to whom I can never be grateful enough for the guidance through which he revealed the world to me in its true nature and truth. Since then, taking responsibility for me, he has watched over me, accompanied me, and helped me learn to see things in their deeper connections. He showed me a path that I still walk, and through it I was able to leave behind my old life that led nowhere and face myself for my own sake. Today I can boldly call the period before meeting him my previous life. It feels as though I did not even live that life myself, as if I were only an outsider watching a film, unable to understand why the protagonist behaves so irrationally, so self-destructively. Now I am grateful to fate for everything—but it was not always so.

My Inheritance

My ancestors have always lived in an ill-fated European country—just as I still do today. My paternal grandparents both came from a very poor rural world. Grandma Rose's family was destitute, so-called mountain people. They lived up in the hills, far from everyone else. My great-grandfather was home only once a month, because the only way to earn money was very far away—far from his home and his family. And they desperately needed money: twelve hungry mouths were waiting for him. My great-grandmother died giving birth to the thirteenth child, though the baby survived. Not for long, unfortunately.

Grandma Rose was the eldest of the siblings. She was fourteen or fifteen at the time. The feeding, tending, and raising of twelve children fell on her shoulders. She could count on no one—my great-grandfather was not with them, and could only come home rarely. She had to carry water from hundreds of yards away, and as for electric light, she might have read about it in a science-fiction book—if they had owned any books at all. In other words, she could barely bear that crushing burden, and she made sure her life became easier. She told the story herself, without a flicker of emotion: how she drowned her siblings one by one while bathing them. One day this one, the next day the other. She spoke about it as indifferently as if she were saying she took out the trash. But she couldn't manage the two oldest, because they were already too strong for her to simply do away with them. I don't know how she did it, but she made sure no one ever discovered what happened to the others. The two surviving siblings eventually lived to old age. You have to remember we're talking about the 1910s and 1920s, when such things could still remain hidden.

Grandpa Rose—who never revealed a thing about his youth—married my grandmother, who, after the horrors of her own childhood, did not want children at all. Yet her life unfolded differently than she had planned. At thirty-seven—an age considered very late in those days—she became pregnant with my father. To put it mildly, she did not take the news well. She did everything she could to miscarry; murder had not troubled her before. And yet my father was born anyway, and within a few years, his two younger brothers followed. With a mother like that, their lot was a childhood starved of love, harsh, abusive, and full of deprivation. Grandma Rose was a malicious, spiteful, envious woman all her life. I was nine when she died, but until then we lived in the same house with her. Because she hated everyone—and my mother most of all—I couldn't expect anything good from her either. She tormented us wherever she could and never hesitated over her methods. She embittered my life, and I did not mourn her when she died. I know that sounds cold, but it's the truth. Today I understand that she, too, was a victim of her own terrible childhood, and I have learned to pity her for that—but it does not absolve her of what she did. Forgiveness, however, I am capable of now.

My fondest childhood memories are tied to Grandpa Rose. In our family and in our circle, people had a very poor opinion of him, but I loved him. He was the only one who had no expectations of me, the only one I didn't have to please, the only one who accepted me as I was. He was a headstrong, free spirit with a fierce sense of justice, and he was never afraid to speak his mind and fight for it. He didn't care what people thought of him, or what others believed was proper. I liked that about him then. I still do. In my earliest memories he was already retired, and I remember how every morning he went out to shave men and cut hair in people's homes—he had been a barber by trade. Because of World War II he lost his barbershop while still young, and was forced to work in a mine to support his family. After retirement he returned to his original calling as a traveling barber. I remember he had many clients, including people who were ill or physically limited. He took me along more than once, and I am deeply grateful, because as a very small child I learned that people in need aren't meant to be pitied—they are meant to be helped. His attitude, so exemplary, shaped me. He didn't judge them. He didn't treat them as "different." He handled them as he did any able-bodied person. He didn't lament, he didn't recoil, he didn't try to solve their lives for them unless they asked. And so they respected and loved him. It was good to see the gratitude in their eyes when Grandpa arrived. He didn't only do his work well—he always had a kind word for each of them, and he often spent hours in their homes. When I was there with him, I loved listening to them. I think those visits, even for a short while, helped him forget his own troubles. His life was hard, and it showed. Home, in any case, was not a calm place where he could recharge—it was a battlefield. Grandpa could not forgive Grandma for betraying him and cheating on him more than once during their life together. They fought constantly. And I, as a child, had to watch that madness. Sometimes the pot—with that day's lunch still in it—flew out the door. Other times Grandma did.

In those days, women were beaten often. Some days Grandpa chased Grandma and hit her; other days my father hit my mother. There was something for every day. With us, jealousy didn't usually turn violent without a reason. I don't want to go into who did what and why. You could list the arguments for and against forever, but the answer to that kind of problem is never physical violence. Whatever anyone believes, brutality is unacceptable in any relationship. Thanks to my wise mentor, I have learned since then that it is never acceptable for someone to live like a slave under another's rule. It is not acceptable to be lonely in company. It is not acceptable that one person has everything and feels fine while the other is barely treated as human—whether the one who suffers is a man or a woman. Unfortunately, it is most often women who suffer these things. Violence, aggression, and any other form of abuse must not be accepted, endured, or treated as a natural part of daily life. Only a weak, contemptible, foolish person abuses loved ones—or any fellow human being—when they have no other tools left to solve a problem. Of course, there are smarter ways to handle conflict, but my parents and grandparents did not have the inner resources for them. I was not physically abused, but the emotional and mental abuse I endured made me hate the whole situation—and the helplessness. I could do nothing, yet I had to watch and live through the traumas they caused me. Today I know that the roots of every problem reach into childhood, and that a child is truly fortunate if she can grow up in a loving, gentle, supportive family. Mine, sadly, was not like that. I hated being a child. If I look at the man-woman dynamics in my family and environment—the ones that shaped me—then it becomes easier to understand why my own marriage turned out catastrophic. It isn't surprising. I saw constant conflict, always someone fighting with someone over something. And far too often it ended in violence. I never had a good example in front of me—because my ancestors' lives were not good examples either.

My maternal grandparents' lives were no model for me, either. They lived in the poorer part of town, which was really a miners' colony. Grandma Mary's childhood was a nightmare too. Her family was so poor that her parents sold her at the age of three to a traveling circus. After that she went with them through the countryside, from city to city, village to village. As a tiny child she had to learn what work was, what hunger was, what it meant to be unloved. She endured a whole catalogue of abuse. When, a few years later, the traveling circus pitched its tent again in her birth village, relatives recognized the little girl—thin to the bone, worked to exhaustion, unwashed, and in rags. They took pity on her and bought her back from the circus. What happened to her parents, where they were then, no one knows. No one spoke of it—no one told her, either. Mad, isn't it? After that, her life was still not easy: the relatives were poor farmers too. But at least she belonged somewhere. Even as a child

Grandma Mary knew what it meant to be cast out, and she bent to pick up every crumb of affection. She was a decent, hardworking girl, who eventually married Adam, my grandfather—a butcher who had once been respected and well-regarded, but had fallen on hard times. He was a very gentle man, but an alcoholic. Grandma drank, too, to drink the liquor before he could. And if that didn't help, she sometimes gave Grandpa a thorough beating. It doesn't take much imagination to picture what their daily life looked like: a toxic relationship, with all its misery. From all this it's clear that my grandparents did not pass down much in the way of healthy value. Their children were my parents. You can imagine what kind of life my parents were set up for—especially in their life together. So what could I have expected?

My parents were children during World War II. My mother, Regina, was born in 1939, the middle child between her older sister Margaret and her younger brother, Adam Jr. Their childhood was very hard, because the family was deported because of their origins, and they lost almost everything. During the war my grandfather Adam was taken by the SS through forced conscription. He fought on the southeastern front and eventually fell into

Russian captivity. Not long before the war ended, he managed to escape with five companions. During their flight they had to cross a minefield. One by one, the five men beside him exploded— only Grandpa made it across alive. The road home still held countless hardships, yet he did make it home. Everyone considered it a divine miracle. Even before he was captured, in a trench he had made a small reliquary out of a spent cartridge casing, with a tiny statue of Saint Anthony inside. The whole family was certain that this was what helped him survive the minefield and return. I still have that relic to this day, and I carry it with me always. From that point on, Grandma Mary became a regular churchgoer out of gratitude to Saint Anthony for watching over Grandpa. My mother was deeply grateful too. She didn't attend Mass, but every time she passed a church, she went in and dropped a small sum into Saint Anthony's box as an offering. She did this even when I was with her later, so it became a tradition in our family.

During the war Grandma Mary had to care for the three children alone. She had no income at all, so they lived on charity. If relatives hadn't supported them with food, they would certainly have starved. At one point a Soviet soldier even lived with them for a few months, and that was how they got food from the Russian rations. After the war they were given a tiny one-room flat in a miners' colony. They had almost nothing, so five people shared a single bed. They slept with one person's head at the other's feet. After the war things did not improve much. Grandpa did get work at the mine, but inflation was so severe that sometimes, by the time he received his pay at the end of the month, they could buy only a single loaf of bread with it. So that the family could at least eat, Grandma Mary went out to do farmwork for others; that brought a little vegetable to the table and a bit of extra money to survive. The three siblings walked four miles a day, there and back, to school. My mother told me that in those times of deprivation she often had to stay home because she had no shoes, and in the cold she couldn't go to school. She also told me Grandma could only wrap a small piece of bread in newspaper for their snack, and it would crumble to bits in their schoolbags. My mother remembered that Grandma didn't care much about her children. She never played with them, wasn't interested in whether they did well in school, or where they were all day. She spent most of her time at the neighbors'—where the accordion never stopped, and people drank and danced. The neighbors loved Grandma for her party spirit. My mother, of course, didn't like it, but as a child she could do nothing. In return she scolded her mother constantly. My mother was also terribly bothered by the fact that there was no wardrobe in the flat and no curtains on the window, because Grandma had no desire for such things. So around the age of thirteen she was forced to take on the mother's role; Grandpa supported her in it. He persuaded her—since in those days there was no other way—to apply to mine management for wardrobes and beds. Of course, the cost was deducted from his wages in monthly installments, but that was how they finally had furniture and could sleep in separate beds at last. When my mother was fourteen her hands swelled completely after crocheting, over eight months, a lace curtain for a four-yard-wide window so that prying eyes from the street couldn't look in. Until then, nothing had covered the window. And yet, despite everything, she still said she had a good childhood because she was free—she could go where she wanted and come home when she wanted.

My father was born in 1937. Grandma Rose gave birth to him at thirty-seven, after an unwanted pregnancy. He was the firstborn son, Alex. Two more sons were born after him: Joey and Jonny. My father, too, was given a difficult and sorrowful childhood. His mother struggled to accept that, contrary to her plans, she had children after all. So she blamed my father for everything and held him accountable for every misfortune. On top of that she constantly turned Grandpa Rose against him, which resulted in regular beatings. He was beaten even when his younger brothers misbehaved—which happened often. Joey was a little devil, a true troublemaker. Always getting into trouble, like any combative, aggressive boy who looks for a fight. When he went too far, he would run home, hoping my father would protect him again, as he had so many times before. And each time, he did. He had to—because if he didn't, Grandpa would punish him. Sometimes—more than once—it happened that Grandpa tied him to a tree in the yard and beat him savagely with a belt. Perhaps because of the many trials, my father had frightening strength, and he could easily defend his brothers. Many people feared him, even though at heart he was a gentle man. Still, more than a few ended up in the hospital because of him. When it came up, he would say he had never started anything—he had only had to do it to protect his brothers, and he felt terrible about it.

Years later, Joey spent a short time in prison for disorderly conduct, but in the end it wasn't troublemaking that destroyed him. He died young in a traffic accident. He had just turned thirty-three. A careless driver struck him dead when he tried to cross to the other side of the road after dark. He was almost across when an off-duty police officer hit him. Far above the speed limit in town, he was barreling along at eighty miles per hour at the moment of impact. Joey had no chance of survival. He died at the scene. Investigators never disclosed the officer's blood alcohol level, so rumors spread that he had been drunk. Even so, they blamed Joey for the accident; they even dragged up his prison record to smear him. Naturally, the officer was acquitted. That was how things worked then. And even today, abuses like that are not rare. Back then everyone proved powerless against the police, even though Joey was innocent. And the tragedies that struck the brothers continued. Jonny, the youngest, died of leukemia that autumn—the same year I was born. He was only eighteen. The whole family mourned him, because he truly was a good boy. My mother was especially fond of him; he was her real support, the one she could always turn to when she had trouble. Jonny would even stand up to my father if he felt my father wasn't treating my mother right. His death was an enormous loss.

My father worked his entire life at a single workplace. Perhaps that was because he was valuable and appreciated. He was known as a reliable, skilled architectural professional, and the supervision of the most difficult jobs—those requiring the greatest attention—was always entrusted to him. At the local civil defense command he created the evacuation plan for the entire county, in case another war broke out. He gave regular lectures on the subject, and was considered an excellent, charismatic speaker. He received many commendations for his work and for his role in civil defense. And yet he was not beloved by his superiors, because he always stood by his principles and never let an injustice pass without speaking up. My mother used to say my father was an exceptional expert—but also a sucker, because while he could arrange and fight for anything for others, he was incapable of turning any advantage to his own benefit. It is also true that my father received several high-level job offers from private and state companies, but each time my mother produced a whole list of reasons why he shouldn't take them, and in the end she always talked him out of it. I respected his competence and his stamina. I considered it admirable that he always stood up for what was right—but I was also afraid of him, because at home he behaved like a military commander: strict, distant, and stone-hearted.

My mother grew into an exceptionally beautiful young woman, and she kept that beauty well into old age. People generally liked her because she could find the right tone with anyone; she was kind and helpful. She was surrounded by many male friends and suitors. According to her, her beauty—combined with her cheerful personality—made her the center of attention. She met my father through one of her friends. They moved in some of the same social circles, but at first my mother didn't like him. She thought he was too serious and stiff, barely smiled, sat in the corner and didn't talk much—just watched. It happened more than once that she had my father drive her to her next date, taking him so little seriously.

So she turned him down several times, and in the end, in 1956, my father traveled abroad with a few friends in heartbreak. He kept in touch with his parents by letter and wrote to them why he had gone off into the world. He wrote that he would never return—except in the one case that my mother became his wife. After that, Grandma Rose kept sending messages to my mother: call him home, what will become of us, who will take care of us when we're old, because Alex is the family's support. They emotionally blackmailed her, saying she was selfish if she couldn't do even that much. They tried to bribe her too: she didn't have to marry him, just promise, and once he was home she could break up with him if she wanted. The pressure on her was enormous; they set everyone they knew on her to get what they wanted. So, unwillingly, she contacted him. My father couldn't express his feelings well in speech, but in writing he could, and he sent my mother beautiful, heartwarming love letters and postcards. I read them too; they truly were beautiful. In one letter he wrote that he didn't want to come home and asked my mother to go abroad to him instead—to build a family there. My mother, of course, had no intention of living abroad, so she wrote back that she would marry him only if he returned. In the end my father came home only because of her, and she married him because she had promised. That strange, one-sided bond shaped our lives to the end of theirs. Not long after my father returned, they held the wedding. Grandma Rose was not pleased, because that wasn't how she had imagined it. She wanted my mother to disappear once her son was home; she had another girl in mind as a daughter-in-law. She tried to split them up, but by then my parents had committed to each other. My father loved my mother with his whole heart when he married her—that I'm sure of. My mother's feelings were less certain.

After that, because they didn't even have enough money to rent a small flat, they moved in with my father's parents. They could not have found a worse solution. Grandma Rose sabotaged them wherever she could. She hated my mother and made sure my mother felt it constantly. My mother was in shock when she realized what kind of family she had fallen into. There were constant fights escalating to physical violence, constant cursing, humiliation, degradation—abuse at its highest pitch. I was born a little more than half a year after my parents moved into the Rose house. I came into the family in the summer of 1959— little Hilda. I, too, received much the same welcome from Grandma as my parents had. My father's family, my mother used to say, was hell—and from what I knew of them, I agree. Looking back, I never understood why, when they finally had the chance to move out, they stayed. My father urged it, but my mother always canceled the move, and in doing so—without intending it—she kept us in an intensely abusive, poisonous environment. The poverty, the constant conflict, and Grandma's endless scheming destroyed my parents' relationship. My father wanted the move to end that cursed state of affairs and give us calm conditions, but my mother insisted on staying. Later I understood: she always wanted to please everyone—as if I were looking into a mirror—and she may have believed that if she endured it long enough, they would eventually accept her and love her. Meanwhile she neglected my father completely on an emotional level; she either had no strength left for that, or perhaps she never knew how to express tenderness toward him at all. I suspect the latter, because I remember very few occasions when they hugged, or when my mother stroked my father's hand back. So after a time—though my father loved my mother—he looked for a woman who would give him the attention and gentleness he needed. That, of course, did not remain secret, and it became fuel for a new wave of fights. My mother threatened divorce; my father threatened suicide. And so everything stayed the same. My mother constantly provoked and goaded my father, and my father— unfortunately—was sometimes a man of deeds rather than words. Then, sometimes, he hit her. I always felt the absence of any sense of emotional belonging between them. Both fled into work to escape the problems at home. They came home only when they absolutely had to, and they left me alone. I don't believe it ever crossed their minds what I thought of them, what example they were setting, what I might be feeling. And yet they deserve undeniable credit as well: even if they could not support my emotional development more—because they themselves lacked emotional maturity—they gradually fought their way out of the initial destitution through inhuman amounts of work, and they provided me with a comfortable life. They taught me to struggle, to fight for my goals. For that I am profoundly grateful.

That is, I think, more than enough—perhaps too much—about my ancestors. In recent years, thanks to the growth I have achieved, I can now easily recognize the origins of my own life's crises in the lives of my grandparents and parents. Because what kind of healthy emotional life can someone live—and offer their children—who murders her siblings? Or someone who is sold as a toddler? Who is to blame for that? Whom do we accuse? Ourselves? Our parents? Our grandparents? Our great-grandparents? Even earlier ancestors? Where do you even seize the beginning of the chain? I'm not saying that despite everything my ancestors didn't want to be good parents—and yes, they could have learned from their own parents' mistakes—but they didn't. Just as I didn't, for a long time. So I'm not surprised that my life, too, went so terribly astray—until the nearly fatal incident with which I began my story. Since I was very small, I felt and knew that the way we lived was not life, because life isn't like that. Life is beautiful.

Looking back at my child-self, I drew a rather strange conclusion about family—and about men and women. I perceived that men loved women, but that women, once they became wives, did not love—or could not love—their husbands. For some reason the relationship didn't work. It seemed to me that husbands and wives never understood one another, and that men therefore sought the company of other women, because in that relationship they were happy. I speak from experience: my father, my grandfather, and my husband all had mistresses for decades. Today I know how flawed those conclusions were. I had no idea what would await me when, as a child, I mused that when I grew up I should find a man patient enough, experienced enough, rich enough in feeling, to teach me everything necessary to make a man happy. I would prove it could be done. My husband would not need to seek happiness elsewhere.

I was wrong—how wrong. I did learn how to make the man I chose—the man who became my husband—happy. But I lost myself completely. In time it turned out he was neither experienced nor rich in feeling, and that he had not married me out of love—though before our wedding he hid that carefully. Or perhaps it was simply that I didn't want to see the truth. Looking back, the signs were there, right in front of my eyes. I didn't want to see them, and so I made the wrong decision. That was part of the self-deception. My mother drilled into me from the time I was tiny that men must only be loved from a distance, because every one of them wants only sex. She waged a whole smear campaign to frighten me away. She had plenty to worry about: already in first grade I was head-over-heels in love with a boy in fourth. The fact that this became an object of ridicule in my family is another matter—and it caused many later problems. Our extended family—parents and grandparents included— lived an emotionally barren life. I cannot recall a single instance when one of them expressed a positive feeling and received a positive response. They simply didn't know what to do with any manifestation of warmth. And so they could not show me how to handle it, or how to speak about it. That created a situation in which, although many boys were interested in me, because of my upbringing I could not express what I felt for them. My husband was the first man with whom I could let myself go. I never imagined then what a terrible direction that budding relationship would take—and that my marriage would become a nightmare for me.

Much later, in my new life, when my eyes finally opened enough to understand, I was shocked to realize how a girl could ever develop healthy confidence when her mother and/or father stuffs her full of their own fears and inhibitions. This is precisely one reason men and women so often relate to sex differently—women, very often, are inhibited and prudish. And of course, truthfully, there are few men capable of dissolving those inhibitions in a woman. The only real solution is to break the chain somewhere. Beyond the influence of the environment, parents carry enormous responsibility. Their task is to send their children out into the world emotionally stable, equipped with self-knowledge, self-confidence, and self-respect—so they can approach one another as equals, as human beings. So they know there is no hierarchy—no above and below—at home, at work, on the street, in any traffic situation, or in life at large. Everyone's work and life matter equally, whether one is a doctor and the other a housekeeper, a truck driver, or someone raising children at home. I deliberately avoided gender distinctions, because a doctor can be a man or a woman, a housekeeper can be a man or a woman, a truck driver can be a man or a woman, and the parent at home can be a man or a woman. We should not distinguish among ourselves by sex or any other inborn trait, but by our actions. One person is human, and so is the other. Parents are responsible for raising children to understand that. No child should grow up being underestimated, intimidated, emotionally and/or physically abused, neglected, dismissed—at any level. No one should forget where they came from, what they once promised their child-self: that they would do this or that differently than their parents did. Or what good their parents did that they want to pass down to their own child one day. If only I had understood this earlier—then I, too, would have been a better parent.

You can blame anyone you like for your fate, but only you can do something against it. Only you can save yourself—this, too, I have learned by now. Of course, it usually doesn't happen without help. I consider myself fortunate—more than fortunate—and I consider it an infinite honor that an Angel became my mentor. His existence reaches beyond the boundaries of reality, and it is as unbelievable as the fact that, right where I live, life guided me to him—and guided him to me. Today I know exactly why. With his help, and through persistent work—learning from my ancestors' mistakes and my own, drawing the proper conclusions—I was able to steer my life in the right direction. Because of this, my life's path can serve as an example and can advance the greater aims he carries. So I managed to change my ill fate. Anyone can. You only have to truly want, with heart and soul, to step onto that road—and if you must, to seek a true helper. If you do not look, you will never find one. If you search with a pure heart and unwavering will, then fate—or God, whichever you can accept—will lead you to the place and the person appointed to help you, called into being for that purpose. That is what happened to me.

For a long time I searched for myself and got nowhere. I realized I would need help if I wanted to succeed. After years of steadfast searching and countless disappointments, fate finally led me to the otherworldly helper I had been waiting for all along. Again and again, through the inner growth he guided me toward, it proved true that I had to remember my child-self if I wanted to do anything with my life. What did I want to be then? How did I imagine my adult life? What would I do? When would I feel good? Did I want a family—and what kind of family life did I picture for myself? What have I done well so far, and what must I change—and what have I gotten terribly wrong? Life is a series of decisions, and a single wrong one can send you light-years away from your original goal. You have to want—really want—to find your way back to that original purpose, so that fate will place an opportunity in your path, something you can cling to in order to reach it.

My Upbringing

When I was born, mothers had to go back to work after just a few weeks. That was true for my mother as well. There was only one problem: back then there were no daycares. Everyone solved it however they could. Since my paternal grandparents—the ones we lived with—would not take responsibility for watching me, my mother had to walk every morning at dawn, in snow and mud, a full mile with me in her arms, to my father's relatives—my godparents. They watched me until my mother finished her shift. Then she ran home, lit the stove, and came to get me. My parents were very poor. No one helped them with anything; they had to produce everything by their own strength. Their survival required unbelievable diligence and ingenuity. They both worked with every ounce of their power just to get from one day to the next. So my relatives watched me; they lived close enough for that to be possible. They had no children, and it seemed they couldn't. They loved me very much, and after a while they didn't want to give me back to my mother. Their reasoning was that my parents couldn't raise me anyway, because they were so poor. With them—my godparents—I would have a much better life, and everyone would be blessed if I stayed. It turned into a massive fight. My mother lost it completely. She was outraged that they tried to take me from her by exploiting her trusting nature. Her maternal instinct rose up, along with sheer defiance: she would show the family that yes, she could raise me. She quit her job and stayed home until I was three, no matter how hard it was to live on one paycheck. Of course that earned her the relatives' anger. Then again, they hadn't respected her to begin with, so not much changed. According to my mother, they always watched her and checked up on her—whether she fed me enough, what clothes she dressed me in, whether she was raising me to be polite, and of course what my grades were. But they couldn't find fault with anything, because as far as my mother's caretaking went, no one could reasonably complain. The truth, though, is that because my godparents watched me—and raised me—until I was eight months old, my emotional bond formed with them, not with my own parents. So later, no matter how my mother tried to build that bond with me, she no longer had a chance.

She never let go of her idea of what I was supposed to be. She didn't grasp—like many parents don't, as I myself didn't when I became a mother—that a child is a separate person. You're meant to help that person unfold, not turn her into a puppet shaped to your expectations. That fundamental misunderstanding created endless conflict between us. In her own way she truly tried everything she could, but after a while she gave up. We never truly managed to attach to each other. And because the conflict also distanced me from my godparents, there was no one left who could have been my emotional anchor. Perhaps that, too, contributed to my later, underdeveloped emotional intelligence. My extraordinary mentor gave me the greatest gift a person can receive: the chance to understand myself. It took his wisdom, his humanity, and his boundless patience—because even for him it was a serious challenge—to bring me to the point where I could speak about my feelings at all, where I even had words to express them.

At three, I started kindergarten, and I loved it. I felt good there. I liked being in a group with children my own age, and I absolutely adored Miss Nanny. You couldn't help loving her. She was an enchanting, kind, always-smiling fairy of a woman. She spent so much time with us. Our kindergarten was beautiful: a huge shady yard with horse chestnut trees, a little garden pool, unusual playground equipment, climbing frames. It was wonderful fun. Usually Miss Nanny was with us, and because she gave me so much attentive care—which I missed desperately at home—a special bond formed between us. The district where we lived had once been its own settlement before it was annexed to the city. In my childhood it still had the feel of a closed community, where everyone knew everyone, and because we lived at one end of the village and the kindergarten was at the other, every blessed day we had to walk through the entire place. We walked a mile to kindergarten, which meant there was time to look around, pick flowers, pet cats, and greet neighbors. A story survived in the family as an anecdote: once, when I came home from kindergarten, I went into my parents' bedroom, where there was a big mirror. I stood in front of it and, in a sweet little imitation of the grown-ups, began declaring loudly, "Just like her mother, just like her father!" My parents nearly split with laughter. They found it hilarious, because half the village knew my father and the other half knew my mother. Since I myself thought I could see a great deal of resemblance between them and me, I wasn't surprised by strangers' reactions. They didn't know that I wasn't proud of it at all—quite the opposite. I didn't want to resemble them, and at night I cried quietly in my bed, wishing I could leave this place. That would take on tremendous significance later in my life.

I think comparing children to their parents is common in every family, and ours was no exception. In my view it's a very bad habit, because it exerts a powerful subconscious influence on children and makes it difficult for them to find their own identity. And it certainly doesn't strengthen positive traits or build self-confidence if you constantly hear, "You're as violent as your father," and "You're as fussy as your mother." The examples are endless, and I think almost everyone has encountered comments like that in childhood. What settles into a child's mind is that she is "bad" in this way and that, that her actions and behavior provoke negative feelings in the people around her. Gradually she values herself—and her own actions—less and less. Not to mention what kind of picture forms in a child's mind of her father or mother if the parents constantly label each other with negative words. I remember a later, fierce argument with my father. I no longer remember exactly what we were fighting about, but my father only kept shouting that I should not be like him. I was stunned. I shouted back, furious, "Then who am I supposed to be like—the mailman? Set a good example, and then I'll know what's right!" That took him by surprise. He said nothing. He only bowed his head in shame.

Sadly, there was no one close to me who could have served as a model worth following. But when it came to practical knowledge—how to function in life—they passed that on to me masterfully. It's true my father did not spare me; he treated me as if I were a boy. He even used to say, when I rebelled against the heavy work, "You're my son and my daughter. You have to be able to take it!" He taught me almost everything he knew. I had to do my share of every job. He was an architect and a true jack-of-all-trades, which meant that sooner or later I had to be competent at everything. I built a wooden cabin, from measuring and cutting to staining to assembly. I drilled a well with a hand auger. I poured something like two hundred concrete posts. I worked on cars, repaired locks, glazed windows. I learned to weld, to prune, to spray, to dig the garden, to store vegetables in a cellar, to cure meat, to smoke it, to care for animals—and I could go on. From my mother I learned the arts of running a household and managing domestic work, of handling money and economizing. She was careful about our ecological footprint long before that phrase—and everything behind it— had even been invented. She taught me to sew, knit, crochet. She made sure to draw my attention to keeping a clean home and good personal hygiene, and she took great care with our appearance. In those chores she tried to spare me as much as she could, but if I was home and my mother didn't give me work, my father would certainly find a "suitable" task for me.

As a child I suffered under this, because they could communicate with me only through work. "Shared experiences" meant working together. Both of them had exceptional organizational skill and were therefore extraordinarily efficient at whatever they began. I inherited that trait from them, and I consider it a blessing, because it makes my life far easier. I could—and can—

solve complex tasks with what looks like ease. Thanks to it, I have overcome many damned hard situations. But the occasions when time together existed purely for my joy, purely about me, were very rare. Still, there are a few I remember with a full heart. When I was very small, every spring my father took me to pick snowdrops. A month or two later, to gather violets, and very rarely, to hunt for mushrooms. He and I both loved nature. He knew how to move through it as if it were his own living room, and so those outings were a pleasure—being with him, going with him. He knew the forest like the back of his hand. Together we listened to the woodpecker's tapping, watched the squirrel carry food into its hollow. Sometimes we found the wild boars' wallow. We climbed the hunting stand to spy on the deer as they raided the corn. He noticed everything, so we often tracked animal prints, or he showed me a grass snake resting beneath a mushroom cap. Very rare, very beautiful memories. Aside from those moments, we didn't go on hikes, we didn't lounge in the backyard, we didn't picnic. There was no such thing as useless time. There was only work. With immeasurable energy, creativity, and determination they fought to prove that anything can be achieved if you want it badly enough. And for that lived lesson I am grateful. My father's guiding line still rings in my ears, the one he would repeat when I was discouraged or about to give up: "My girl, you can't give up. You're a Rose girl. The Roses never give up." I don't agree with many of his methods; some I oppose outright. But that sentence has been a tremendous support to me to this day, and that attitude followed me all my life.

School

Starting first grade was, for me, a miracle. I loved it—every aspect of it. I wish every child could have a teacher like my first one. She was endlessly patient, kind, attentive, as if she had stepped out of a storybook. And that is where the good memories end. At the beginning of second grade our class got a new teacher, and she stayed with us through fourth. If only she hadn't. I spent my first four school years in a small elementary school that served only the lower grades. The principal had a service apartment right there in the schoolyard, in a separate little building. Which meant we played out there during recess, right in front of his home. So the principal's life was an open book to us. And what I saw left a sour taste in my mouth. For instance, my new teacher began a secret affair with the principal, and they seized every opportunity to make use of the times when the principal's wife wasn't home. More than once I saw the teacher come out of his apartment still tugging her skirt into place and smoothing her mussed hair. I found her hypocritical, because while she did that, she expected us to look at her as the very statue of morality. She preached constantly about respect and couldn't understand why she didn't receive it from us. After I told these things at home, my father spoke to the principal and told him to restrain himself, because the children could see what he was doing and the whole thing would end badly. From that point on, the teacher's behavior toward me changed noticeably. She became malicious and sullen. And that was how my first four years of elementary school passed.

In upper elementary I went to a different school, but my luck with teachers didn't improve. There it wasn't one problematic teacher—it was half a dozen. Of course there were refreshing exceptions. One was my history teacher, who also ran the school's community life. She was a teacher through and through. I think of her with gratitude to this day. To her—and only her—I wrote a thank-you letter forty years after our paths separated, moving her to tears, though the honor was mine, being her student. In general I've never been very good at hiding what I feel. If I form an opinion of someone, it shows on my face immediately. That's what happened with my homeroom teacher too—the one who taught us three different subjects. At the time I simply thought the teaching profession wasn't for him, so I was quite dismissive and sarcastic toward him. And it was written all over my face. After one parents' meeting my mother came home desperate and tried to appeal to my conscience, because my homeroom teacher had complained that whenever I looked at him, my face always displayed the expression, *you're an idiot*. Over the years, our relationship did settle down, because his approach to teaching changed, and he took part in a great deal of community work, cooperating with us. By then I was already in love with poetry, and I tried writing poems myself. There were pieces he read aloud in class and then put up on the school bulletin board. And because I liked performing, he always prepared me whenever there was a school event where a poem had to be recited. Studying, though, was a struggle. I loved going to school, but I didn't love studying—or rather, not everything. I adored literature, history, music, and art history, but I didn't like the sciences at all. With the teachers I had, that isn't surprising. By then I was already training in gymnastics, which helped with my high school entrance, because by that time I was a national champion. My academic record wasn't necessarily a glowing recommendation, but since what was starting then was the county's—or perhaps the country's—first physical education track, where they wanted to gather the region's best, most successful athletes, there was no question that the gymnastics team would be accepted as a whole, and so I was too.

In high school, already in the first year, we were held in high regard. Our class was made up of national champions and national-team competitors—people who excelled in both individual and team sports—and we carried the confidence and spine that comes with that. It's no wonder that at our first national high school sports competition we won everything we entered, across every sport. Our school became known throughout the country. Its prestige and reputation soared, and so our standing was high as well. Even studying went fairly well. I didn't fall behind, I cleared the obstacles, and a truly good community formed among us. But, as so often in my life, that pleasant state didn't last long. In the second year we were given a new homeroom teacher—a male teacher of math and physics—who became a nightmare for most of the class. I had to get up every morning at six because the school was far away and transportation was poor. And for that same reason I couldn't even go home after classes, because I wouldn't have made it back for gymnastics practice. Practice ended at eight in the evening, I got home around nine or nine-thirty, so my entire day was occupied. Because of competitions, I couldn't rest on weekends either. And on top of that, as a result of practices that ended late and weekend meets, I couldn't sleep at night. It's no wonder that I lived in constant exhaustion and fatigue. And as if that weren't enough, our new homeroom teacher hated athletes. He didn't take our workload into account at all, and he made our lives miserable wherever he could. Along some peculiar line of thought he developed the delusion—one he voiced regularly—that athletes didn't belong in high school, because they weren't serious enough about studying. They only wasted their teachers' time and energy. He threatened us that he would show us—none of us would graduate from that school. In his first year he systematically made life impossible for the ones he disliked. It went so far that the parents of several classmates transferred them immediately to another school. I didn't have that luck, and I suffered through three years. Many times I got such stomach cramps before math class that I had to go home. He humiliated me so often, and to such a degree, I can hardly even describe it. And I—like an idiot—let it happen. I bowed my head. The saddest part is that my parents let it happen too.

Today I would do it differently. I wouldn't let it go. But in those days teachers were surrounded by enormous respect. Sometimes he showed his human side, though it didn't leave a deep mark on me, and it didn't undo anything. That wretched state reached its peak at the end of the fourth year, when he failed several of us for no reason, so that in the end we truly could not take our final exams. Later, of course, I passed my final exams without any trouble at another school. That says a great deal about him. That is how certain teachers, through petty behavior, can destroy a child's future. I had to wait until our thirtieth reunion for his apology. He admitted that I wasn't such a bad student that he should have done what he did. What happened between the two of us is a living example of how one person can ruin another's life without the other having given any reason at all. He took a year from my life and ruined four. How do you make that right with an apology? You don't. Perhaps with actions, yes.

Life

After I graduated, I stayed home for a year because I wanted to apply to the local teacher-training college. Since my teens I had wanted to be an elementary school teacher. I believed that high school teachers taught fixed material—math, literature, specialized subjects—whereas elementary teachers could teach what they wanted. I thought they had far more freedom in educating children than subject teachers did. I wanted to teach children how to live. Of course, no higher-education program includes a course called *How to Live*. But I wanted to reform teaching, because I didn't like what I had experienced in the school system at all. I missed—and I still miss—that school does not prepare children for life. During that one year of preparation, I learned more than I had in the four years altogether. In history they couldn't have asked me anything I couldn't have given at least a short lecture on. At the entrance exam I began with history, and I did excellently. In literature I knew every topic so well I could have recited it in my sleep. There was only one topic I didn't learn, one I didn't read. It was the work of an author I didn't particularly like and found difficult to understand. I'll be honest: I had no idea what his work was even about, because I didn't understand it, and the teacher didn't put any energy into helping us understand it, so it didn't interest me at all. It was completely beyond my abilities. And I promised myself that if I drew that topic, I wouldn't struggle and I wouldn't ask for a different one. If that happened, then I didn't need to go to teacher-training; I was meant to go elsewhere. Naturally, that was the topic I drew. Needless to say, I did not become a teacher.

After that, for a while, I drifted without aim. Then an opportunity came up, and I completed the assistant gymnastics coach training and the gymnastics judging program. For two years I worked as a volunteer coach at my former gymnastics club, without any pay at all. I received a great deal of encouragement, because they were very pleased with me. I was promised that as soon as a position opened up, I would be hired as a paid coach. I was thrilled. I loved working with children, and I poured enormous energy into the job. There were times, at nineteen, when I took a group of six-to-eight ten- and twelve-year-old gymnasts on my own to competitions in distant cities. I arranged the travel, lodging, meals, competition accreditation—everything—entirely independently. And meanwhile I was at practice every single day. During that period I completed the coaching program at the college, because I felt this was my path. Of course, it didn't end as a happy story. One day I was walking into the gym for practice, and what did I see? Two former teammates—girls who had never coached, who had never even stood beside a child to assist, not once. They hadn't completed the coaching track either, and yet there they were, helping with my students. Management told me they had reassigned me: I should work with the injured athletes, and with those who needed lighter training. I was stunned. My former coaches— who had by then become my fellow coaches— apologized again and again and said it wasn't their choice. "Someone" had placed those girls there. They couldn't do anything about it. But I shouldn't worry: next time a spot opened, it would be mine. There was no next time. I left immediately. They stabbed me in the back where it hurt the most. I took it so hard that for more than thirty years afterward I couldn't even watch gymnastics on TV.

I had no idea what to do, so my father arranged for me to be hired as an administrator at the company where he worked. It was supposed to be a temporary replacement job, but then they made it permanent. First I was assigned to the cash office, then to accounting. For that, however, I had to complete a secondary vocational program in economics. Even though I had a diploma, it wasn't a vocational diploma. That was what they required, so I became a certified bookkeeper, corporate planner, and statistician. But it soon became obvious to me that bookkeeping—and especially employee life—was not my world. Not at all. I love varied, lively work. I can't stand being closed in, staring at numbers all day. No creativity. For me that place was hell. What was very good, though, was that I gained that knowledge at all, because later I was able to use it successfully in my own business. In the meantime, I got married. When the baby came, I stayed home until she was three. When I would have had to go back to work, my mother suggested something: what if we opened a flower shop in the apartment building where, at that time, I lived with my then-husband and our little girl. By then we no longer lived with my parents, because through my workplace we had been given an apartment. Not for free, but on very favorable terms. It felt like a miracle. A four-story building, second floor, two rooms, a small balcony. Our own little kingdom—plus a garage.

In the basement of that building there was a small grocery. Its owner—who had once worked with my mother—kept urging her more and more firmly to take over the business. My mother refused to hear of it. She didn't want to be a food merchant again. I wanted it very much, because as a child I had loved being in my mother's shop, and I had dreamed of having such a store myself. No matter how I tried, I couldn't persuade her. My mother pictured a flower shop for herself, and in the end she persuaded me instead: we would take a floristry course together and buy the little shop, and we would sell flowers. And that's what we did. Based on my mother's wonderful interior designs, my father—assisted by me—remodeled the shop with remarkable skill and beauty. And we opened. It wasn't a gold mine, but my mother adored it. I did not, at least not in the same way. I liked dealing with people, but floristry wasn't made for me. It didn't make me happy. In the end, because of our constant friction, we couldn't work together. So my mother withdrew from the business, and the shop was left to me. For a while

I kept the flower shop going alone, but then the income of my customer base shifted, and my revenue fell so low that I had to change. First I began selling fruits and vegetables, and then, after a full transformation, my wish finally came true. I had a grocery store. After endless planning, measuring, thinking, coordinating with tradesmen, and overseeing the work, I opened. I loved every minute of it. For the first two years I did everything alone. The bread and pastries arrived at four-thirty in the morning, and I had to be there to receive them, because if they were simply left in front of the store, I was robbed every single time. After that I went to get milk, and at six o'clock I opened. At noon I closed for one hour; I cooked then, or washed laundry, or ironed. Then I opened again until six in the evening. After that I went out for goods, brought them back, and stocked the shelves. When I finally closed, I still had to care for the family—dinner, the child, everything—and then I collapsed into bed. I have no idea how I managed it. I think love of work drove me forward. I made a ton of money, but I worked an insane amount. There were times we went away for a weekend to rest at a hotel. We arrived, went up to the room, I lay down—and I slept both days straight through. I didn't have the strength to go downstairs to eat.

But after that rest returned some power to me, I rose again like a phoenix, and everything continued.

It could have gone on forever. We kept growing. My husband, after a while, earned well too. And with that, our desires grew as well. I wanted a family house. He wanted a new car. So I didn't spare myself—just as he did his share of earning. In the end we bought a huge plot of land, where we cultivated grapes and fruit, and where we began building a house. But the division of labor between us wasn't equal. I took on far more than was fair, and my appreciation was equal to zero. That is what broke me. Growth mattered to me, too, not only to him—though our intentions were completely different. Both of us were driven by greed. I knew he cared only about money and property. I cared only about him, so I was capable of anything if it would make him look satisfied. I sacrificed twenty-two years to make him happy, and I hoped that if he was happy, then we—my daughter and I—would be happy too. That moment never came. After the divorce, he asked me, genuinely surprised: if he had been happy, how was it possible that I hadn't been? Our house was finished. We had moved in perhaps a month earlier. One evening we were getting ready for bed when the usual hide-and-seek began. He got up and went out into the garden as if he still had something to do. I did, in fact, still have things outside. When I went out, I saw it: in the dark, behind a bush, the glow of his phone screen, and he was whispering into it. Something in me was done. I felt an immeasurable sorrow. When he came back into the bedroom, I was already in bed. I sat up and asked him, in a tired voice, why he had to make phone calls in the dark, hiding behind a bush. I will never forget the moment—his face—how contempt, laced with disgust, spread across it, and in a twisted voice he shouted at me: what did I, pathetic as I was, have to do with his life? He would do whatever he wanted. I stared at him, stunned. But inside me I felt something snap—literally. Resigned, I only said that he was right. I had nothing to do with it. Then I laid my head down on the pillow. And I heard bells in my head. Whenever I set some significant change in motion in my life, whenever I made a right decision about something important, bells rang in my head. It was a marvelous feeling. I slept the calmest night of my life. In the morning I knew immediately: the first thing I would do that day was begin the divorce.

By the time I reached that moment, I could no longer bear the tension that had accumulated in me over decades, tension created by my compromises. The traumas of my childhood, neglect, the feeling of not being understood, the lovelessness of my marriage, the emptiness of my whole life up to then, the constant hunger to please—when you do everything you can to be accepted, respected, loved. And yet you meet constant rejection, expectations beyond your strength, and nothing is ever good enough for them to accept you, respect you, and above all, love you. That was enough, in that moment, for me to give up there on the road, facing the truck. Thank God, my sense of responsibility for others saved my life. I would not have forgiven myself even in the afterlife if, with my stupid decision, I ruined a man's life—the truck driver's. Up until that moment I believed I could only love myself if I received confirmation from someone else—if someone finally said, *You're good. You're enough. I love you exactly as you are.* That moment—while I was steering my car into the path of the truck—was when I realized I was my own greatest enemy. I understood I had to learn to love myself, because only after that would others love me too. That was when I jerked the wheel away and stayed alive, so that I could share this as a lesson with others. I needed the closeness of death for my eyes to finally open.

It's true: my former husband's belittling, contemptuous, repulsive sentence gave the decisive push that made me start the divorce. And yet even then, five years had to pass from my suicide attempt until I was free. But it's also true that none of this would have been enough for my life to take a new direction—and for me not to repeat my mistakes. I am certain the turn would not have succeeded if I had not received help from above. I have traveled a long road, and I am grateful to fate for every minute—for giving me a chance to change. But I will never be able to thank my mentor enough for helping me close my old life and giving me a new one in its place—one of value. A life I build with my own hands, but whose foundation stones he laid. The self-knowledge, the courage, the clarity without which I would not exist today. He showed me that it isn't only possible to survive—it is possible to live. Truly, with a whole heart, open toward myself. What my mentor did was more than mere help; it carried me toward a kind of rebirth. He gave me a gift beyond measure, one that cannot be repaid—only passed on. What I learned from him is no longer only mine, and perhaps one day I, too, can be a light for someone in the dark.

Marriage

December 6, 1981 was a cold, snowy winter day—the day of my friend's wedding. And I didn't really want to go. I felt awkward about showing up alone on such a happy day, and spending the whole evening dancing only with her father, whom I did love very much, but that is not what a young girl dreams of. I thought I would die of boredom among so many strangers, most of them my parents' or grandparents' age. I went only so I wouldn't disappoint my friend. She was waiting for me, counting on me. They had paid for my dinner. It would have been rude not to show up. I didn't even prepare for the big day. Under other circumstances I would have gone to the hairdresser, bought a new dress, dressed my soul in celebration too. This time I simply shoved my fur hat onto my head, pulled on a thick wool skirt, my sheepskin coat, my felt boots, and walked down to the church about half a mile from our house, where the ceremony was being held. I told myself it would be thirty minutes, then I'd go home, change clothes, and then take the bus and walk into the city center to the wedding reception. Back then I had no personal style of my own. I only tried things on, or let other people influence me. And so I arrived with a terrible hairstyle and clothes that were completely wrong for the occasion. When the ceremony ended, I was standing at the church entrance, waiting for the newlyweds to come out. That was when a tall, handsome young man in military uniform stepped up to me, with an irresistibly charming smile. I have to admit, he looked damn good. He asked whether I was the bride's friend. I said yes. He told me he was a friend of the groom, and we introduced ourselves. He wanted to know whether I was going to the reception by car. I told him no, I would take the bus. There was still room in his car, so he offered to drive me. As we spoke, the groom's parents pulled him aside and began talking to him with intense emotion. While they did, he kept glancing at me with an anxious look. When he came back to me, he apologized and explained that the groom's parents had asked him to drive the grandparents to the civil ceremony hall, and unfortunately that meant I wouldn't fit in the car. I could see he was genuinely embarrassed. I reassured him not to worry about it. In any case, I had to go home first to change, and only then could I leave. He offered, then, that he would come back for me—if I would just tell him where I lived. He made one or two caring little remarks, and they touched my heart in a way no one had managed before. We parted with the hope of seeing each other again, and while he didn't yet know it, I did—in that moment I knew he would be my husband. Perhaps I shouldn't have been so reckless. But even today, in certain situations, that impulsiveness is still part of me—though I have improved. I went home, and the moment I stepped through the door, I announced to my mother that I had found my husband. She nearly fainted. She began questioning me in shock, but I brushed away all her concerns. I was utterly convinced it would be so—and so it was. Congratulations to me.

It was as if I'd been hypnotized. I went to the wedding reception with an unquestionable, overwhelming certainty. All evening I was so calm, so balanced, so sure of myself that even the people sitting around us thought we had known each other for years, that we had been a couple a long time. Looking back at our conversations and his behavior, I don't think he felt anything like that at all. But it flattered his vanity that I was so taken with him. He told me that a few months before we met he had broken up with his fiancée because she had cheated on him. In hindsight, in the way he spoke about it, she was the great love of his life, the one he never forgot. I was only an instrument of revenge and proof. He seized the opportunity to prove to his family—through me—that although he had let go of a rich girl, he had found another, one who lived even better, because by then my parents, through their relentless work, had accumulated real wealth. So I met a criterion his family considered essential. Hypocrisy was not foreign to his personality, so it wasn't hard for him to convince me that he was the kind of man I had always been searching for. And I wanted to believe it. I wanted to believe he was my prince. Very late—far too late—I realized that I had simply draped him in the qualities I considered important in a man's character. The reality was light-years away. It wasn't his fault that I didn't notice. I clung to my dreams and refused to face the possibility that I might be wrong. Today I see clearly that we should not have married. I should have broken up with him, but I didn't. It was a mistake. I think I wanted to prove it to my family—and to myself—that I would succeed. And I wanted so badly to escape my home life that marriage seemed like a wonderfully attractive decision. The hope that he would become a good husband, and my blind faith that he would eventually be what I had always imagined, never became reality. The attentive, emotional, cooperative, caring boyfriend—who seemed to recognize the other as an equal—gradually turned into an insensitive, incapable-of-cooperation, sly, arrogant, pasha-like husband who swept every problem under the rug. At the beginning, when he was still in the army, he wrote to me almost every day: love poems, syrupy lines. He found a sweet little pastry shop that became our regular place, and he always said that when we were old there would be one spot filled with tender memories. He bought theater subscriptions because he knew I loved going. There was always a pleasant surprise for me. He knew how to be kind in a way that mattered to my soul. When we spoke about the future, he always wanted what was good for me. It seemed we had the same values. Seemed. Because in truth, he wasn't agreeing with me—he was simply hiding his own opinions and thoughts. That is a very different thing. It became clear later that his motivation for our relationship was something else entirely. He convinced me he loved me, though he never truly did. He loved my parents' money. That, very much.

I look back on our wedding day with a bitter taste. He came to pick me up at my parents' house. His cousin and the cousin's wife drove him; the car was decorated. They came in, spoke a few words with my parents. When I came out of the other room in full bridal splendor, glowing with happiness, I expected that when he saw me he would say something kind, touch my cheek, or hug me. I was stunned that from a respectful distance all he asked was whether I was ready. I will never forget his eyes. As if he were being led to his execution. In that moment I knew I should not marry him. I was a breath away from going back into the room, taking off the dress and the veil, and ending this play. But I didn't, because I was a coward. My compulsion to prove myself and to please others was far stronger than my self-respect. I no longer ask myself what would have happened if I had stopped it then. Life doesn't work that way. I chose that path. No one held a gun to my head and forced me to marry him. It was my wrong decision. We went through with the wedding, then the reception—but it was not the happiest day of my life. I am convinced it wasn't his, either. He was tense the entire day, visibly uncomfortable. He didn't compliment me, he didn't indulge in tenderness. He did the assignment, and for him the matter was closed. And I, as usual, manufactured explanations for his behavior. He must be overwhelmed. He isn't used to so much attention. He's reserved. He's tired. And so on. In truth, he was only the obedient child of his parents, desperate not to disappoint them. He would have experienced it as a failure if he couldn't pull this marriage off. For his parents, wealth was terribly important, so they raised their son to find a rich girl. That was what mattered to them, and he wanted to be their good boy. He thought then they would love him. He had a great deal of disappointment ahead of him. My husband received from me all the love, attention, and care he should have received from his parents, but he kept waiting for it from them. He didn't need it from me. We chose marriage for different reasons, but our shared compulsion to please gave birth to a bad decision on both sides. We couldn't face the fact that searching and choosing is not shameful—it is vital, because we are looking for someone with whom we intend to live an entire life. Someone with whom we want to build a family, have children, make a nest, take care of each other. How are we supposed to do that if we don't believe in it from the beginning? How many people are like we were—people who compromise and make the wrong choice? Choosing a partner is one of the most important resolutions and decisions of a life. Only after long consideration, with real firmness and self-knowledge, should anyone form a partnership. But what do we do instead? We fulfill our parents' dreams and desires—because they want grandchildren. Or we prove to our girlfriends that we, too, have been "taken" and become wives. We run away from home because we think that will solve everything. And I could list more. I'm not saying every marriage and relationship is bad. But you rarely see a balanced, happy marriage. Not because no one wants it—everyone wants it. But most people, when they choose a partner, are not yet grown. They are still children. And most remain so to the end of their lives.

A Child Is Born

When I became a teenager and imagined my future—my future family—I could imagine it only within a relationship. I believed a child absolutely needs a father, a father's example. I wanted a big family, because I had no siblings, and I missed that terribly. It would have been good. It wasn't. In both my father's family and my mother's there were three siblings each. As an adult, analyzing their relationships, I'm not surprised they wanted no more than one. I, too, was destined for one child—one child with whom I had to learn lessons I could not have learned under any other circumstances. I am the type who ripens late and slowly, so it wasn't until around twenty-one that I began looking at boys at all through the lens of what kind of husband they would be, whether I could be happy beside them. There were plenty of suitors, but only my future husband managed to get close enough that I could imagine a life with him. It mattered enormously to me that our views on life, family, work, the division of labor matched; that basic human values—like the sanctity of family, decency, tolerance, gratitude, perseverance, diligence, rejection of aggression—would decisively characterize us both. I always imagined a married couple living life together, fighting side by side for each other, and sharing its joys. That was the kind of man I wanted to bear children for. But it remained only a dream.

The man I chose presented himself as a partner in everything. Based on his attitude then, he could have been my twin—he wanted what I wanted so completely. I couldn't say anything to him that didn't earn the answer I wanted to hear. And that was the problem. He said what I wanted to hear, and I didn't notice that it wasn't coming from his heart—it was only a way to obtain something. Not to obtain me, in truth, but the comfortable life accessible through me. He asked whether I liked children. When I said yes, he immediately said he did too. If I wanted four children, he wanted five. He would support everything. He would teach them everything, we would take them everywhere, we would go play soccer, go fishing! Yes. Just the way you imagine it. But I didn't know that then. I became his happily—though I found his approach to having children strangely unsettling. We talked about it, yes, but I imagined the time hadn't come yet. Perhaps deep down I felt he wasn't the ideal partner for it. I only note this: by now I've learned that the "ideal time" never arrives. You begin when both people are ready—not to satisfy future grandparents' wishes, not to submit to outside pressure. I was his ringed fiancée when he began persuading me not to use contraception, to let a baby come. At first I refused even to hear of it, but he was so overwhelming, so relentless, that I gave in. I didn't understand the urgency—after all, we weren't even married yet. But I was already so in love that I couldn't say no. From that point on he threw himself at me as if his life depended on it. And I did not want it. It was emotionally crushing for me that sex wasn't about mutual joy—it was like compulsory homework that should have been turned in yesterday. It served only the purpose of conception. I didn't want to live it that way, but by then I had surrendered my right to decide for myself. I let events carry me. Looking back, it dawned on me why he pushed for a child so hard before the marriage. He knew I would never leave if we had a child.

For the first nine months of our marriage we lived in a house my parents had given us. Not long after the wedding, I conceived. My pregnancy was highly problematic, so I was on medical leave after the first exam. The first half of pregnancy exhausted me. In the fourth month I developed horrific kidney spasms. The baby lay on my ureter, causing unbearable cramps. I tolerate pain well, but this was unendurable. I asked a neighbor to call my husband and tell him to come home because he had to take me to the doctor, who was already waiting to examine me. He came home, he drove me to the emergency clinic—and he didn't escort me upstairs to the office. He excused himself by saying he was in work clothes and he wouldn't get out of the car like that; I should go up alone. I could barely move, folded nearly in half, and he left me. He watched me limp and drag myself up the stairs. And just as then, later too, neither I nor the baby moved him to real concern. The pain became so strong I was hospitalized. They tried to reduce my suffering with medication and IV fluids. I am a disciplined, easy patient; I don't fuss. But with that monstrous pain I screamed and cried out so much they eventually put me in a private room. There was a risk they would have to terminate the pregnancy, because my life was in danger. I could only hope for the best. Eventually the spasms began to ease, and to everyone's great relief, I was soon able to go home.

After that I didn't dare risk staying alone in our house all day. Other complications arose during the pregnancy too, and there was a fear I might need urgent intervention at any time. We asked my husband's parents for help, but they refused, rigidly. My mother, on the other hand, welcomed me with open arms. My father had reservations— not without reason, because by then he had already read my husband correctly. I am grateful that despite that, my parents helped us and we could move in with them. Out of their three rooms they gave us one. It wasn't ideal, but I was in a forced situation. My husband, of course, wasn't happy about the change. From the start he had been scheming to reduce contact between me and my parents to the bare minimum. That might have been understandable to a point—if he weren't doing it out of self-interest. For him, it served the purpose of claiming me entirely, alienating me from everyone, and keeping me under control. And yes, I too wanted to separate from my parents. That was one reason I had married. So it was easy for him. But because I received no support from my husband, I threw myself into proving to him that I would do everything for the two of us—for us and the baby. I hoped he would fulfill the promises he had made. That was the story of the next twenty-two years of my life—completely fruitlessly. A great mistake.

The second half of my pregnancy, aside from minor troubles, went smoothly. It was a very happy period. It was an extraordinary experience to feel a new life growing inside me. And my little baby performed incredible stretches. I loved it when I could trace her limbs through my belly as she moved. Perhaps she couldn't imagine why she was bundled into such a small space, so she kept trying to expand the room she had. Toward the end of August my contractions began at home. Fortunately our neighbor was a midwife; she helped me through the panic and told me what to do. By the time I went in for the third test of the amniotic fluid, the frequency of the contractions already suggested that this would be birth. My doctor examined me and sent me straight to the preparatory ward, then to the delivery room. That was all he did—though I paid him plenty. What followed has a name now. Obstetric violence. Fear, loss of dignity, helplessness, abandonment, loneliness, powerlessness—those were the hallmarks of my entire labor. I was placed in a situation I felt I could not manage alone, and instead of understanding and support I received only inhuman treatment. That made my birth violent and traumatic. I don't know what experiences others have had with childbirth, but with the mind I have now, I would report that doctor and the entire hospital for the humiliating, inhuman way they behaved. I wanted my husband to be present and help me, but the hospital rules at that time didn't allow it. I suspect that even if it had been allowed, he wouldn't have come in. So I was alone. I had to do it alone. I panicked. Fear took over. I did not want to live my first birth like that. I was left completely to myself, with no idea what would happen. I was terrified the birth would truly begin and no one would be near me to help. I couldn't even wipe the sweat from my forehead, or moisten my cracked lips with a wet cloth. There was nothing and no one—only, beyond the curtain dividing the beds, the loud moans and cries of other women suffering beside me. The nurse who came once an hour answered no questions normally—if she answered at all. It's a mercy my labor didn't last long, because although my whole body was locked in fear and I wasn't dilating at all, the pushing urges grew stronger and stronger. Finally I was given an injection that loosened me enough that the birth could begin, more or less. At five-thirty in the evening I was taken into the delivery room, where they practically pressed the child out of me. Imagine the situation: the doctor kneeling on my abdomen, pressing his full weight into my ribs so the baby couldn't slide back, while the midwife between my legs tried to catch the baby for the same reason. She did not want to come out, but at 10:10 p.m. my beautiful, healthy baby was born. I was infinitely happy. My husband was immeasurably disappointed, because instead of a boy, it was a girl.

A wonderful, peaceful feeling took hold of me. It's a pity I had to experience it alone and couldn't share it with anyone. When I could finally move, I could barely breathe for days. The doctor's brutal intervention likely fractured one of my ribs. The crushing pressure had another consequence too, bringing pain so intense I hovered constantly on the edge of fainting. I couldn't walk, I couldn't sit. I didn't understand how the other mothers could stroll cheerfully up and down after giving birth while I was nearly out of my mind, at death's door. After I came home, it was the midwife neighbor who examined me and helped me understand what was wrong, and how to remedy it. To my great sorrow, I couldn't breastfeed either. In the hospital the nurses gave the babies so much tea before feeding time that my little one was never hungry; she slept through the feedings. That meant I should have pumped milk, but because of my condition I could barely manage, and the hospital conditions were not suitable. In those days, if a woman had such a problem, she was in trouble. I was too. By the time I got home, both breasts were inflamed. With a fever above 104, aching ribs, and no strength, I lay at home helpless. The inflammation was so severe that the possibility was raised they might have to remove a breast. I went for regular checkups. I had to ice them. I was given antibiotics, which meant I couldn't breastfeed—while my baby girl screamed herself hoarse with hunger. It is a heart-rending feeling when your tiny baby is hungry and you, her mother, cannot nurse her. And on top of that, she refused every formula. It was a nightmare. I felt I was losing my mind from helplessness.

When a woman has her first child, the taboos around birth and sheer inexperience make life brutally difficult for the family—especially for the mother. And yet I am unspeakably grateful to my own mother for the way she nursed me in those hard weeks after birth. She took every burden off my shoulders. We still lived with my parents after the delivery. With careful attention she tended me, and she cared for my daughter too. She did everything I couldn't do because of my condition. In time she enjoyed being a grandmother so much that once I recovered, she no longer wanted to step back. She sensed the growing tension between my husband and me, and—whether consciously or not—she used it against us. At first she sweetly offered, if it wasn't a problem, to take the baby so we could be alone. The next time she suggested we leave the child with her and go somewhere together. Eventually she practically chased us out of the house, claiming we should go do our business and earn a lot of money, because we needed it now, and she would watch the little one. What began as a good idea and real help later poisoned the relationships in the entire family. My husband already tried to stay away from the family—just as he stayed away from his own daughter—so he was not a partner in building an independent life. For him the situation was downright convenient, because he didn't have to deal with the child. And again, I was alone. I tried to reclaim my daughter, but I wasn't strong enough to stand up to my mother, who always achieved what she wanted through the false illusion of good intentions and the usual emotional blackmail. Slowly she drove a wedge between me and my daughter, and we still carry the consequences today. I continued my mother's pattern: where her godparents had obstructed the emotional bond between mother and daughter, here my mother, as grandmother, obstructed the bond between me and my daughter.

Today, of course, I would do everything differently. Because now I try to live by new principles given to me by my mentor, among them this: "One of the highest aims of a human life is to educate oneself into being a good parent, and thus pass on one's inner values to one's children." So I learned that raising a child begins with planning to have one. Why do I want a child? To satisfy grandparents' desires, or from my own inner call? Do I want to realize my dreams through her, or do I support her in becoming fully herself? How important is it to show love and faith in her, to put myself second at times, to practice renunciation, sacrifice, mutual respect? Do I understand what parents' obligations are—obligations they willingly take on when they bring a child into the world? These are unavoidable, vital things everyone should think through. Thanks to my mentor, I can now see how much I did wrong, and how much I could have done for my daughter that I did not do. Sadly, you cannot start again. In many ways I was not a good mother, though I wanted to be, and I did everything I could. My greatest mistake was that I let others direct my life, and for a very, very long time it stayed that way. I wanted to satisfy everyone, but I could not give my little girl more love, attention, and understanding than I had received. I gave her, emotionally, what I had been given by my parents—practically nothing. The enormous amount of work, the chase for money, the urge to please my environment and above all my husband drained me so completely that only crumbs were left for my child. Materially she had everything, but emotionally I could give her very little. It's understandable that she is emotionally more attached to her grandmother than to me. Nothing will change that now. She is an adult. I can't turn back time. I can't choose a different father for her. And I can't throw my mother out now, when she wormed her way into our life and took over. I didn't do it then because I couldn't do more. At that time, that was the extent of what I was capable of—just as my mother and father couldn't do more, either. That was the extent of them. That was what we had to build with.

Now I know life is about how I use what I experienced and learned in childhood—and how I make up for what was missing, where and how I can fill it in. Do I recognize what is right and worth following, what is wrong and should be rejected? Do I plan my life accordingly, and fight? I have principles now, and I never give up, no matter what happens. I believe I am here on Earth to learn and to grow. Perhaps I have learned the lesson. Every day I see the example of how to do it—how it should be done. Now I can only hope that my daughter learns from her parents' mistakes, and that when her children grow up, they will pass a kinder judgment on her.

The Anatomy of Love

For me, the feeling of love is a cataclysmic experience—akin to what a person can know only in the nearness of God. When we were born, we lost the sensation of existing in everlasting happiness. Perhaps the teachings of various churches—that eternal happiness is in Heaven— are true. With one difference: I don't call it

Heaven. I call it returning home into God. People seek love because they seek eternal happiness. But the feeling of love is not eternal. It is temporary. Very few people experience it steadily with one partner, over the long haul. What happens to us in childhood damages, in astonishing ways, the chances that human beings can form and sustain a healthy relationship that lasts a lifetime. And yet that was exactly the intention with which I entered my marriage. That it failed depended on many things. Twenty-two years had to pass before I admitted that I could not do more for my marriage—and that I no longer wanted to. Enough. Twenty-two years. You couldn't say I rushed the decision. I am, by nature, a fighter. It was hard even to confess to myself that it was a waste of steam, that this ship had sailed—or rather, that it had never been there at all, except in my imagination. It is highly likely that my inadequate upbringing and limited emotional education were the reason I did not recognize the violence done to me within the family—violence that did not show itself as physical assault but as psychological terror. That sly, intangible, almost invisible psychological ambush: they find the weakest point in your soul and they attack it continuously, from childhood onward. I won't say you get used to it, because you don't. My weakest point was probably my compulsion to please. I wanted to be good for everyone, to be the good little girl, so that amid all the fighting we were used to at home, at least there would be no trouble with me. And even then, after a single defiant moment, my mother—who was a master of emotional blackmail—would push me away by saying she didn't love me, or by threatening to disown me.

As an adult, long after my father died, it happened once that for some reason I didn't call my mother for two days. When I finally did, she demanded explanations with outrage and tears, trying to blackmail me emotionally by saying that for all I cared, she could already be decomposing. Then later came my husband's methodical, insidious passive aggression, which succeeded in grinding my confidence down to zero. At first it was only small, "funny" jabs, little remarks. That was how he communicated his expectations—about my behavior, my clothing, the way I spoke. It extended to how I looked, how I laughed, how I cooked, how I baked. But no matter what I did, no matter how hard I tried to please him, it was never enough. There was always a new demand—without the smallest sign of appreciation for what I had already done. Only the mistakes and the shortcomings were ever brought up. If I spoke up because of it, or if I didn't do what he expected in that moment, he punished me by withholding attention. He didn't yell, he didn't argue—he simply didn't speak. He looked through me, treated me like air, left without a word, went out, didn't pick up the phone, didn't call back. If I wanted to talk, he always found an excuse—most often he mentioned my menstrual cycle. Other times he would say, condescending and arrogant, that I should leave him alone, and what did I even want to discuss—there was nothing to discuss. And then he would simply walk away. Later he began avoiding me openly. If he was in the kitchen and I went in, he would go into the living room. If I followed into the living room, he went into the bathroom. I thought perhaps our relationship would be strengthened if we took more long weekends away together—thermal spas, somewhere to relax. Unfortunately, there was never any gratitude in it. If we were in the room, he watched television or slept. If we went to the pool, he treated me like air and chose some woman to stare at, or he withdrew with his phone and spent long hours "talking about work with a female colleague." It drove me mad. At the beginning of our marriage I trusted him completely. I was never jealous. If he had any program at all, I encouraged him to go. There were times I picked him up by car at one in the morning after a party with coworkers. I trusted him entirely—and he abused that trust. In the early years it wasn't like this. Back then he worked as a lathe operator in a factory. It wasn't his world; he hated it. There he didn't come into contact with other women, but that situation changed soon enough. Because he complained constantly that he hated his job, I persuaded him to finish secondary school, to earn his diploma, so he would have options and wouldn't have to bury himself in a factory. During those two years, while he studied, our relationship deteriorated further. Our little girl was already a year old then, and in our two-room apartment we had to tiptoe as if we lived in a museum, because everything disturbed him. Most of all, perhaps, our very existence. That is what it felt like.

He had already finished school and passed his exams when we were at his parents' vacation cottage and one of the neighbors came by—a man they had kept up a friendship with for years. I make acquaintances easily, and I like talking to people because I'm curious about them, so we were soon in conversation. I didn't know what he did for a living, but somehow the subject came up. It turned out he was the head of the court enforcement office. One thing led to another, and in the end I asked whether he might be able to secure a job for my husband. When I want something badly enough, I can usually make it happen. And so I arranged a position for my husband as a court enforcement officer—so thoroughly that even the neighbor felt honored to employ him. My husband's joy was endless. He became tremendously proud of himself because, of course, he credited the achievement to himself and his parents—after all, it was their acquaintance, not mine. Typical. For them, that old acquaintance would have remained a drinking buddy until the end of time if I hadn't pushed, if I hadn't asked for help. They had known each other for more than ten years and yet it occurred to neither of them to make use of the opportunity. Still, I received no gratitude for it. Not even that. I didn't say anything. I told myself it didn't matter; it stays in the family. The point was that he could leave the factory and there would be no more whining. He would be in a good place. For the first month or two, during training, he earned a near-starvation wage. Later he couldn't complain. Enforcement officers made very good money in those days, and that sort of work caused my husband no moral crisis whatsoever. But along with it, the problems arrived too—in the form of women. And the husband I thought reliable could not and did not want to resist them. He stayed out more and more. He always found a reason why he had to leave earlier, come home later, disappear for days, go on vacation with colleagues. At first I accepted it. Then came the female intuition, and then certainty. His mistresses walked up and down in front of our house and rang our bell, telling my husband to come out to them. Nighttime phone calls became regular. If I happened to answer, they hung up without a word. If he answered, he usually got into the car and left. It was humiliating. Of course we fought constantly.

Now I know what a fool I was. What was the point of the fighting? It only made everything worse. I should have tried to talk through our problems. Only he did not want to speak with me. Yes—the best decision would have been to leave. But my little girl was there. In the end, what could I have done?! That question will be familiar to anyone who has lived this. I lived in the belief that I had no choice. It was easier to shift responsibility somewhere else. And so I remained the foolish woman I was. If I could stand in front of my former self now, I would shout at myself to wake up and see what was happening around me. Since that is impossible, the three of us suffered on. During our arguments, he always deflected by saying I wasn't normal, that I must be going crazy. He insisted I had no reason to be jealous, and anyway I shouldn't pester him without cause—his job was like this, and people contacted him only because of work.

After a while I found myself questioning my own sanity. I sank so deeply into that condition that I reached the point where I began to see myself through his eyes. I believed him: that I really was a wreck, an unfit mother and wife, and that I was incredibly lucky this decent man would put up with me, one way or another. And it is typical that instead of understanding, your environment treats you as the source of all problems. Without the smallest trace of empathy they question your mental state, claiming that you have it so good you no longer even know what's wrong with you. Abusers always try to isolate their victims from family and friends. That happened to me too. He cut me off from my friends completely, always made remarks about them. Then he would press himself close to me and ask with sorrowful eyes why he wasn't enough for me, why I didn't do things with him instead. He accused me of caring more about my friends than about him. Nonsense. And yet I canceled invitation after invitation, sitting at home waiting for my "loving" partner to appear and spend his precious time with me. I could have waited forever. If I complained, the response was that I shouldn't expect him to spend all his time with me. He had better things to do.

To the outside world, however, he always showed his best face—his most devoted, kindest, most attentive mask. Everyone around us believed I had hit the jackpot with this man, that we were a perfect couple. Yes. A perfect nightmare. And I am partly to blame for that illusion, because I learned too how to perform for others and show our "nice" face. When he felt he had gone too far, he spent more time at home, the sweetness returned—flowers, and the "I love only you" blah-blah. And I always believed him, because I wanted to trust him. I believed him even when I knew he was going on vacation with another woman. Or when his mistress divorced because of him, and he paid off the woman's husband after the divorce with our money. It is astonishing how deep a person can sink, how many terrible forms self-harm and self-destruction can take. Anyone who has lived the darkest depths of loneliness inside company— daily humiliation, constant blame, contempt—

knows what I mean. If I complained to my mother, she always quieted me: this is a woman's fate, don't rebel. My husband was only like that because I was always "hysterical." He was such a good man, I should appreciate him. I could expect understanding and support from no one, so I had to find some kind of solution myself— and in my final desperation I nearly chose wrongly. Instead of my daughter, I chose a truck. I am ashamed, in front of her, of my selfishness. My parents' lives and the lives of everyone around me—relatives, neighbors—were, to put it mildly, far from the ideal I had imagined. I believed that if I married, he would teach me how to live, because I didn't know. I chose terribly, because he was not the one capable of that. Beyond hypocrisy, trampling others into the mud, and humiliating them, he wasn't very skilled at anything—least of all at feeling love for me and showing it. Because I had no idea what a happy life looked like, it took many wounds, many cruelties before I recognized that no matter what I did for this marriage, I would never be happy like this. I decided I had suffered enough, and I had no intention of continuing. The hard battles of twenty-two years led me to the point where I wanted to die. Thanks to divine providence, at the last moment it flashed through me what an immeasurably foolish thing I was about to do. I defied fate and vowed there at the roadside that I would find the reasons that had led me here, and I would learn to live as I had always wanted to. I was certain that somehow I would succeed too. Without outside help, of course, it would have been impossible. But to be able to ask for help, I first had to recognize my situation, my own role in my life, and I had to want change—want a solution. I bless my fate that I was granted that. I asked, and I received—only years later. First I still had to learn to recognize the false, trapping detours, so that at last fate could lead me to a helping Angel.

Seeking the Path

After my suicide attempt, I began searching for someone who would not only listen, but would also help uncover the reasons—why all of this happened to me, and what I could learn from it. A transformation began inside me. At first I lived it with difficulty; later it became natural. I had to try to demolish my ego so that I could build new foundations. I wanted to face my faults and defeat them. I quickly realized how unbelievably hard this was—if not outright impossible. I began, consciously, to look for opportunities that might give me a chance to change myself. I was always open toward everyone, yet I kept for myself the right to choose. I never committed to any direction—no spiritual current, no religion. I listened willingly to anyone, but somehow I still did not find what I was looking for. Anything could come, if it pointed toward a way out: angel courses, fortune-tellers, astrologers, Tibetan healers, spirit healers, swarms of self-development trainings, feng shui, and I could go on and on. I had so many self-help books I could have opened a library. I searched in many places for the true road, and I met only disappointment. I, too, became one of that crowded camp of people in the esoteric world who call themselves "walkers of the path." With the knowledge I have now, I wish the others would find their way out of that glittering but, in truth, worthless fantasy world that leads nowhere.

It outraged me to see how shamelessly self-proclaimed spiritual leaders exploit the naïveté, ignorance, and often the desperation of those seeking a path. They pile up nonsense and crown themselves mighty incarnate souls, then flood their followers with incoherent, transparent lies, demagoguery, and a swamp of clichés. They organize camps where, for unrealistic prices, they sell people nothing. I don't want anyone to misunderstand me. My problem is not that one must pay. If I receive something of value—spiritual teaching, for instance—it is only right to give something in return. Money is simply the easiest way to do that. We are not in the Stone Age, bartering for everything. And I do not agree with the idea that the only true teacher is one who works for free. The most grotesque thing of all is when a student believes he stands above the teacher and wants to dictate what a "real teacher" should be. It strikes me as astonishing arrogance. Unfortunately, many seekers believe that if a teacher teaches them, it is their natural right. It is not. That would be the basest exploitation of a teacher. Anyone who believes that should take a good look inward. Of course, it is also true that one should pay only for truly valuable teaching. If that were the rule, most gurus would go bankrupt. I gained a great deal of experience, back then, of the sometimes utterly absurd workings of the esoteric community—when I still went to such places. I didn't yet know what I was looking for. I only knew I didn't feel right in my own skin. Whenever I went into one of those groups, they always convinced me that I was not really at fault for what was happening to me. I should accept that I was good, let my femininity blossom, simply bring forth the power sleeping inside me. I deserved happiness. I didn't have to do anything except believe in it. In other cases they advised me to rearrange my apartment according to some esoteric principle, because my restless sleep was due to an underground water vein beneath my bed, or because the chi had become stuck in a corner of the room. And the fail-safe method for getting rich was to write a three-digit number—produced by an astrologer through some "mystical" arithmetic—on a piece of paper and keep it under my pillow for three weeks. And this is not a joke. I went through these stations myself. I truly believed it. I truly did these things.

With the mind I have now, I hold my head in my hands at the stupidity of what I was doing. But that was how I lived my life then. In ninety percent of cases I went home in an elevated mood. I felt damn good, because I received affirmation—they gave me, they said to me, what I wanted to hear. I was good. I wasn't to blame. I deserved happiness, and on top of that I didn't have to do anything, only believe in the power of the universe and trust that everything would be fine. Hooray. For a long time I didn't notice that these events weren't helping me out of the situation I was in—they were pushing me deeper, because they gave me a false illusion of myself. It felt good that, not specifically to me but to the room at large, they were always praising us: you're good, you're beautiful, you deserve the good, and besides, you don't have to take responsibility—"the universe" will solve your problems. How marvelous: I just come here, pay a significant sum, and receive, in return, a nice dose of confidence. For a long time I didn't see that it was a vicious circle. No matter how I tried to change my life, these places and people were not capable of offering usable, working solutions instead of the usual resounding nothing. Because I kept falling into the same traps without any real change. In this way I condemned my life to failure. And there is no exception—no one who chooses this mistaken road of "seeking" escapes that. After a while, though, I had enough of the false praise, and of all the talk about letting go and releasing the power within me. It began to bother me more and more that none of the great gurus could answer a simple question: what do I have to do so that something finally truly happens? I wanted something concrete, because these occasions only kept my spirit alive for a little while. Sometimes for two or three days— sometimes I hadn't even stepped out the door and the effect was already gone. I felt I was on a false road. I wanted to do something for myself, and so I kept searching for who could show me the right way.

I know there are people for whom it is enough to hear what they want to hear—and they will even pay for it. Such people are welcomed with open arms by those gurus to whom it is extremely important what their followers think of them. It matters to them that their words are accepted, that their person is accepted, so they shape their message to fit the expectations of their audience. They always say what their followers want to hear. They use symbols and signs of every kind, simply to reach as large a group as possible. They may seem very mystical, but otherwise they speak nonsense, and the point of it all is to dazzle the crowd so they keep coming back. It matters desperately to them that they are accepted—both they and their message. Insight was followed by action. From that point on I avoided the people and opportunities that used to seduce me with their false light. After that, I no longer belonged among them. I wanted to change, and I wanted true answers from someone who would not tell me what I wanted to hear, but what I needed to hear—no matter how painful. When I admitted that I was willing to face myself, and that I would do everything to change my wrong behavior and habits, those realizations earned me many unpleasant minutes. One of them was my egoism. I cared only about myself, and I looked down on anyone who didn't meet the standard. It took an enormous amount of work to reduce my ego to a tolerable level. But it was worth it, because once I had done it, a deep calm and peace moved into my soul. To do that, I needed this: after long search, I had to finally find what only steadfast, determined seekers can find. A kind of miracle— one that proved to me, at last, that this was not simply another New Age lie.

Little Hilda at one year old

At age twelve, competing as a national champion on the uneven bars (top right) and the balance beam (bottom).

Reciting a poem at a school celebration

Senior yearbook photo, 1977

After saying "I do", 1982

With my beloved Grandpa Rose and my former husband

On a seaside vacation with my two-year-old daughter

The last photo taken of my father, surrounded by our family

Part II

Heaven

My Mentor, the Angel

It is almost impossible to put into words what it means to me to be the student and follower of a person who has taken human form yet is, to me, an angel—and what it means that I was allowed to stand in his service, that he is my mentor. An Angel. Why do I say this? I do not claim it—I know it with absolute certainty. His knowledge is boundless. He sees the course of events years in advance with astonishing accuracy. He reads our thoughts: often we do not even have to voice our questions, because he speaks, word for word, what has already begun to form in our minds—and then answers them. Whatever the subject, at whatever depth, he is able to offer relevant, precise, and irrefutable responses. He speaks of connections most people do not see—indeed, do not even understand—connections that science itself discovers only years or decades later. He knows the personal past of individuals, from the simplest details to the most complex life situations. Through him I have experienced things—unfathomable experiences—that no one would believe except those who already know him. And all this is only a fragment of what defines him. Though he himself has never claimed to be an angel, everyone who comes into contact with him feels it. Not only I, but others he guides as well, are convinced of his angelic nature. He always responds the same way: everyone has the right to think whatever they wish about him. He has shared many stories with me that leave no doubt in my mind as to who he truly is and with what clear purpose he is present. I must speak of things and events that, through the lens of our upbringing and beliefs, must be told in a way that is understandable—and that does not sound like madness. And yet every word I write is true. Not fiction, not fantasy, but reality.

It is no ordinary thing for an angel to exert influence upon humanity through a person who considers himself unworthy of such a role. And yet that is precisely the case here. We encounter similar accounts on the pages of sacred writings born thousands of years ago. In human language, there is no more accurate word for him than "angel." Of course, in everyday life I do not address him as Angel or Mentor—I call him by his name. His modest, withdrawn nature is far removed from ostentation, selfishness, clever posturing, or malice—traits that, sadly, are common among people. I confess that I myself have not been, and at times still am not, exempt from human frailty; but whenever such impulses appear in me, he responds with firm, thunderous correction. He never allows me to judge others carelessly or to think in terms of superiority and inferiority. He constantly emphasizes that all people are equal. Everyone has the same right to equal treatment, to a free and happy life, to learning—and the same rights and obligations belong to all, regardless of gender, origin, education, or material circumstance. He never boasts of his knowledge or his abilities, and yet in any situation he can use them in precisely the right way. I owe infinite gratitude to fate that I could be chosen as one who bears witness. Let my life story stand as testimony for all. The angel I had been waiting for is here. One must live with this opportunity, and the souls who truly long to grow will find the path that leads to him.

Encounter

At the beginning of my step onto this new path, I had one wish. I longed to meet someone who would lead me further along the road I'd already started down—someone who could convey a goal and a truth I could accept. The last guru I went to, after a while, told me, "There's nothing new I can tell you anymore. You don't even need answers now—you need to calm your agitated soul." I think the real problem was that he couldn't answer my questions. He suggested I go learn tai chi. I stared at him, ignorant. I hadn't even heard of it before; I couldn't imagine what it might be. He said it was a Chinese martial art. Only then did it begin to ring a bell—that on TV I'd seen Chinese people in the street making those strange, slow, ballet-like movements. It turned out, yes, that's what he meant. There was just one problem: I had no idea where to find such a thing. Back then there was no internet, no social media—only acquaintances, and acquaintances of acquaintances. In early December I did get a phone number that way, but somehow the meeting never came together. Either there was no group, or there was no room. Then the holidays arrived, and in the end we agreed: sometime in the spring. By then I already had enough experience in that world to know he wasn't my person. I let things rest and waited for a sign. In March a daily paper fell into my hands. I started leafing through it—and I, who never read the classifieds, read them that day. What was the first ad that jumped out at me? Private tai chi instruction offered, and a phone number. Nothing more. I called immediately. A pleasant male voice introduced himself. I asked only two things: where do I need to go, and when?

At the time I didn't yet know I was standing at the threshold of a turning point in my life, but it became clear very quickly that the opportunity fate had placed in front of me was anything but ordinary. It soon became obvious that the person my good fortune had led me to was not merely an average man with good abilities, but far more than that. He was not simply a man, but an entity here for a clearly defined purpose. That he helps those who ask him rise to a higher spiritual level is, in a way, only a side activity. And it's needed—because whatever anyone may think about how advanced and intelligent the human being is, they're mistaken. Our technical progress is indeed outstanding, but if you look closely, the general mental and emotional intelligence of the majority has not changed much since the dawn of humanity.

I will never forget it: I had already buzzed the intercom and was climbing the stairs when I panicked, because I hadn't actually made sure he was who he claimed to be. By the time I reached the landing, horror scenarios were running through my mind—what if I was dealing with a pervert who lured women to his apartment to do God knows what to them. Then I calmed myself down. If I sensed anything suspicious when he opened the door, I would run. Well—the door opened, and a tall, powerfully built, piercing gazed, serious "man" stood before me. He radiated astonishing strength, calm, and peace. My future mentor. All my worries vanished. Okay, I thought to myself, I don't need to be afraid of him—and I stepped inside. Once we were in, he had me sit down and we began to talk, and then he asked why I wanted to learn tai chi. I told him it was because my former teacher couldn't teach me anything new anymore and had recommended that my next step should be to calm my soul. He asked what the cause of my agitation was, and what I had done to remedy it. I told him my life story in brief. Then he said that he works with several people, and if I wanted, he would gladly take care of me too, and alongside tai chi he would also pay attention to my inner development. He didn't push. He didn't persuade. He left the choice to me. He made me curious, and I said yes. From then on, at first we met only once a week, and later more and more often—at his place, along with his other students. Needless to say, learning tai chi came to nothing. Instead, an entirely new world opened up for me.

When I asked him why he concerned himself with teaching a Chinese martial art, he replied that whoever is interested in tai chi has a character better suited to him. Years later he told me that every person he wanted to find, he could reach with the "bait" best suited to that particular person. In my case, it was tai chi. Since then we still haven't worked with tai chi—though I did have the chance to see his skill. True, he never learned it from anyone, but with him that is not unusual. His knowledge in this area, too, far surpasses that of others. So I placed my trust in him—but in my wildest dreams I never would have thought I would end up in such a special life situation, with access to things that are unavailable to others, and for many, unimaginable. Because of human subjectivity and limited capacity, people are not able to teach their fellow human beings—so from time to time a being comes to Earth whose intelligence is light-years beyond human intelligence. In our case, an Angel—who is capable of teaching people by methods he deems suitable, and of initiating changes humanity cannot bring about on its own.

When I came to him, I was already ready to face my faults, my stuck places, my fears. With a pure heart I longed for someone to finally see in me what needed to change—because these things pursued me like demons, and I could not be at peace from them. More than anything I wanted to find myself, to be true to myself, because I knew only then could I finally be happy. Getting to know my mentor brought me something that is not given to everyone—but to me, and to a few others, for some special reason, it was granted: the opportunity that finally made my efforts successful, that allowed me to step out of the typical human fate and begin my real new life. In our conversations he gave unmistakable proof that his abilities were not of this world. In this book I tell only those incidents, those stories, that happened in my presence—or happened explicitly to me. They created such deep changes in me that from that point on there were no more attempts ending in failure: things gained real certainty. I experienced with my own eyes things others only dream about. His piercing gaze was always soothing to me; I felt he could see into me. Many people are disturbed by that. I wanted someone, finally, who truly saw me—who saw what I truly am and helped me get to know myself, who I really am, and helped me put into words what clouded my clarity and held me back from growth. He was completely different from those I had gone to before, and it soon proved itself.

Many said they were afraid of him at the first meeting—almost as if they sensed he was not one of them. Instinctively they feel that in front of him they can have no secrets, that he sees straight into them at once and knows everything about them. In some way people's sixth sense detects him. With a glance he knows who someone is, what they are, and what in their past matters. And he knows well in advance when his phone will ring, or when someone is coming to him. Some find him strange because he isn't a fan of pointless small talk—but he answers every meaningful question willingly, in detail, and with readiness. Even when the questioner hasn't said the question out loud. In conversation it's not uncommon that he answers questions that were never asked—the person is still searching for words to shape the question, and my mentor is already answering, to no small astonishment. Nothing remains hidden from him, because he reads our thoughts. Yet whatever he learns about someone, he handles with maximum discretion, and he never turns it against anyone or uses it for his own ends. It is admirable that no matter what topic he's asked about, he responds at the highest level. In the beginning, along with the others, we challenged him countless times—testing him— but he was always demonstrably and undeniably right, no matter what it was. For me it is deeply reassuring that even so, he does not abuse his abilities; you can trust him completely. I learn an enormous amount from him, continuously. My relationship to people—and to life itself—has changed completely. In another chapter of this book I already wrote about how selfish and superficial I was. I lacked empathy, and my subjectivity knew no limits. Through many, many examples he taught me to judge people and situations more objectively, making it possible for me to be far more balanced. So I don't bite someone's head off if they look at me the wrong way; instead, through proper communication, I try to create a clear situation. Because of this, the other person tends to be much more constructive in a given situation as well.

One of his other students was an important station and test in my inner development. Our initial mutual dislike poisoned our relationship completely. But our angelic teacher did not allow negative feelings to overtake us. He continuously gave us tasks we had to solve together, and the successes we lived through side by side—slowly, but surely—bound us to one another. Thanks to his guidance, the desire to become better human beings grew stronger in us than our ego, and after years of struggle we now seek each other's company with genuine joy. There was also someone in our community who changed after more than twenty years. Through persistent care and teaching, he suddenly understood something—and realized that if he followed what our mentor said, he would have a good life. After many years of denial and then acceptance, he finally reached safe harbor, found the meaning of his life. Since then everything around him has changed radically: he has become a successful entrepreneur and feels comfortable in his own skin. You can sense the change in him in strides of miles. Being able to belong to this community is like being part of a family. Our angel mentor treats every member of the community the same way he treats his own children. It is also so good to be near him because in his presence, existence is marked by an easy, childlike freedom. His teachings and guidance give me stable inner foundations for daily life. His credo shapes my worldview, my purpose, my principles. The path I chose this way serves a more exalted aim for me—and gives me tools to live this faith and to live this wondrous inner journey.

How did meeting an Angel change me? He uncovered the life-defining but flawed principles I lived by, and offered alternatives to replace them. He gave what was missing, he supplied what did not exist—exchanging what was wrong for what was right. He gave me a framework and guidance along which I can live a happier life. No, I did not undergo brainwashing. So how can all this be done in such a way that nothing of what I am is lost—and I don't become a person remade by someone else? In every case, I decided—and I still decide—whether I will integrate the offered knowledge, teaching, guidance, or whether I will exchange something for it. In judging these, both the proofs and my clear conscience helped me recognize that these are true truths. These are not symptom treatments; they eliminate the causes that brought so many problems into my life. Of course it wasn't only my belief system that needed correction and still needs correction. I had—still have—plenty of other gaps in knowledge, in the scientific and spiritual realms alike, and in those hard-to-define matters that give wisdom. The result of my growth is not only that I advance spiritually, but that the problems that embittered my life resolve themselves automatically. As I prepare, as I learn these things, I learn to apply them in my life. I no longer need to ask others for help forever in relationship matters or any other topic. I am equipped with knowledge so that I myself can solve them. In other words, through my mentor's upbringing, I finally truly grow up—I become an adult. Setting aside the foolishness of religions—faith is not the same as religion—and the nonsense of esotericism, I see the universe and the human being within it from a completely new perspective. I no longer build only on faith, but on certainty—where at last I learn and understand where I come from, why I live, and where I am headed. I no longer have to fear things like death or loss. And in the same way, I learn that every problem has a solution—and yes, I can get from A to B. As he says: "Every problem has a solution; the question is whether we ourselves—or others—are capable and prepared to solve that particular problem." He helped me immensely to become capable and prepared.

Now I feel I am able to recognize the complexity of the universe, and because of that I look at the world with entirely different eyes: that everything is connected to everything, and where my place is in this system. Of course I am aware that I still have a great deal of growing to do. My mentor leads me along the path—if I want it, and if I am willing to work on myself. And yes, I know: this difficult road is not for everyone. Not everyone can accept their own faults, and not everyone can face them and eliminate them. I committed myself to change, and so from him I received every help—along with solutions put into practice. I know, and it reassures me, that as long as I need it, he works for me to the fullest.

People judge and brand others very easily; I was no exception. That saying—about seeing the speck in another's eye but not the beam in your own—seems to me to be almost universally true. I feel my development has reached the point where, with the help of self-criticism, I can recognize my own faults and I dare—am able— to face the measure of my ignorance. It is a tremendous amount of work, but also an incredible relief. My energy no longer goes into disguising my shortcomings; it goes into strengthening my positive traits, knowing what I am missing. Everyone knows how much negative things pull a person down, while positive ones reinforce them. I choose the latter now.

My mentor is a tremendous help in this. For more than two decades now he has been working with me—and even now I still have to perform at the same high level. His mentoring is certainly not a right that belongs to me by default. I can go to him anytime and ask for advice, help, or ask questions—he will, in every case, guarantee that he will help, if I put myself into it fully. It's like a watchmaker who is there in his workshop. It isn't important to him that my watch runs. If my watch doesn't work, I go to the watchmaker and have it repaired. The watchmaker doesn't run around in the street, stopping everyone who passes by—"Hey, is your watch working? Do you want me to fix it?" No. That would be unfair to the watchmaker. The watchmaker hangs out his sign and waits: "If your watch is broken, bring it here. I'll fix it." I accepted him from our very first meeting because from the beginning I regularly experienced things that others would consider unbelievable—even impossible. From that moment on I could rely on him in everything. He didn't persuade me. I recognized that this was in my interest, and that I had to work worthily for the result. And if I had merely been repeating, yes-yes, I accept you, it would have become clear anyway. Because however strange it may sound, he truly can see into a person's mind—so he would have known. At first I was not a deep thinker; I was more superficial. But I learned from him that before I speak, I should think. If I don't understand something, I should say so— and then he will explain it, even a hundred different ways if necessary. The point is that I understand.

The Path of Change

Living and growing according to an Angel's guidance is not easy. The point is to live this present life in the best possible quality—and to complete it, in the end, with the best possible result. Its primary function, then, is growth, but not the simple kind you find in ordinary "self-improvement." That is why I committed myself to him. I wanted to become a better person, and this path still makes it possible for me to see—proved again and again—whether I have succeeded, and what has not yet succeeded will succeed. Sadly, I still have many faults and many patterns of behavior that need correcting, and I must change them. But compared to where I started, the distance is like heaven and earth. Because I oppose all religious fanaticism, I was relieved that this was not a community organized around blind dogma—yet it still satisfies the spiritual needs that are necessary for me to move forward. I believed—and I still believe—in the cycle of life and death. I believe that sooner or later, by stepping out of that cycle, I can enter a higher form of existence. I want to be worthy of that happening as soon as possible. I believed then, and I still believe now, that there is only one way: by becoming a better human being. That is what I work on. Between the empty fantasy worlds invented by gurus and the path offered by an Angel there is one cardinal difference. My mentor never says what I want to hear; he says what I need to hear. He never struggles to make me accept what he says, because life will prove it—because it has always proved it—that what he says is exactly how it is. The first thing I—and others—had to admit and understand was that this isn't important to him. It is important to us. I accepted that his style of mentoring is not coddling, not make-believe action. If necessary, he states his opinion very firmly; at times he is harsh, almost stone-hearted, and he cannot be bribed with emotions. And yet he is never driven by self-interest. In the end it always becomes clear that this relentless toughness is guided by deep empathy and the will to help. One foundation of his method is consistency, an all-encompassing attention, and meticulous fault-finding. All of this is paired with uncompromising accountability—and an unshakable intention to assist. The path he offers is fundamentally spiritual, yes: it answers how the world works, what the meaning of life is, what the soul is. But this is not emphasized the way it is in religions or in esotericism, where dealing with supernatural matters takes up the overwhelming majority of the time invested. Meanwhile, human behavior—our way of thinking, and the development of that way of thinking—receives vanishingly little emphasis. A person must develop evenly in every area. I have reached the point where I ask only questions that serve my good. The ones that yield answers that do not make me more, and do not make my life better, I set aside. That power-hungry, contemptuous, foolish woman I used to be— surrounded by flatterers—suddenly learned how to read the world, people, and myself. The more I know, the less power matters. In fact, it outright irritates me now, because I can finally see the shadow side of power, too—and that is a very important realization. It took my "I want to become a better person" attitude, and angelic help.

My mentor's extraordinary abilities became clear to me very quickly. For example, our lives were an open book to him. In connection with anything that has happened in my life, he can recall anything. Once he brought up an event that happened to me in childhood—something only I could have known, not even my parents. I had been going to him for a while; we were talking about the determining effect of childhood, when he asked: "Do you remember when you were five years old—sitting in your bed at night, watching the streetlamp's light through the slats of the shutters, and thinking: if only I could go, if only I could run away from there?" Even now, I become tender when I think of it. I was born eighteen years before my mentor, so he wasn't even here when it happened. We had never met before, we hadn't even lived near each other, and our parents didn't know each other. I had buried that memory deep inside myself, and yet he called it up—this shattering moment. Yes, I remember it clearly: I felt unbearably lonely and sad, and I never told anyone. And yet he knew. In detail, in sequence—everything matched. Then, like a lightning strike, came the recognition and the certainty: he is far more than we are. He never boasts of what he knows, but in that moment the picture assembled inside me. The many unexplainable events, the answers to problems that could be found nowhere else—answers we received from him—suddenly made sense. From that moment on, I never questioned his statements again. And he never gave me reason to. What he said—one way or another—always proved true. That was when I decided for good that this is the road I want. I want to work on myself, to be the best person I can be, and to be worthy of representing this to others as well. It was the best decision of my life. It gave me knowledge, backbone, peace—the inner state I had always been searching for. Here I could finally unfold. This was the path that led from being lost to finding my way home. If only everyone could be given this feeling.

Of course, there were times when he set before me tasks so difficult they felt nearly impossible—truly humanly punishing. I will never forget the time our country's government returned churches to the denominations, and those churches, almost as a first step, shut them all down; they were no longer freely accessible. I was outraged to my core. How do they imagine this? There is no reason, no explanation, that could have entitled anyone to do such a thing. Those churches were built from money gathered by our ancestors—most often through the community's volunteer labor—through blood and sweat. Where do they get the nerve? For clarity, let me state: I am not a follower of any religion. But I do have faith, and I believe in God, and for that reason I visited—and I still visit—whatever churches happen to fall in my path. These are God's houses, and God belongs to everyone. By what right do they take from me the possibility of connecting with Him? I completely lost it. I cursed everyone I considered responsible—meaning the leaders of the Catholic Church. I told my mentor what was hurting me. He said, "Why don't you go and tell them?" I stared at him, stunned. "Me? Tell whom?" "Well then, let's go, and you file a complaint with the archbishop. He is the national leader of the Catholic Church." I drew my neck in as small as I could. I wanted to hide, or swallow back what I'd said—but then I realized he was right. If this disturbs me so deeply, then I should do something about it. If I don't, then I should keep my mouth shut. Still, it agitated me terribly. My mentor said that if I went, he would come with me and support me. The situation with the churches offended my sense of justice so strongly, and I didn't want to look like a mere loudmouth—and it calmed me that he would be with me—so I didn't think long. I immediately said yes. I'll go.

A few days later we got into the car and set off. I was driving, but I was nervous and frightened the entire way—almost terrified. After a hundred and sixty miles, we arrived and parked, then walked toward the gate of the archbishop's palace. The palace was a huge, stunning building, with a main entrance that could not be opened from the outside, and an intercom beside it. I was so tense that if I'd been alone, I would have fled.

But he was there, encouraging me. "Go on, ring the bell. Or are you afraid of something? What could possibly happen? Worst case, they send you away—and then you're off the hook. The question is: what do you want? To do what you came for, or to fail?" Well. If we had come this far, I couldn't betray myself. So, come what may, I rang. After a moment the gate opened. Behind it stood a security guard who, upon seeing my mentor, was more flustered than I was. He asked what our business was and whether we had an appointment. I'll be honest: it hadn't even occurred to me that I should make one. So I said we didn't, but I wanted to lodge a complaint with the archbishop about the closure of the churches. At first he hesitated—then, as if bewitched, he stepped into action. He told us to wait a moment; he would handle it. He called someone, and that person told him to escort us upstairs. As it turned out, the archbishop was out, but the head of the archdiocese received us. We walked down a long upstairs corridor of the beautifully renovated building; about halfway down was the Chancellor's office. A sweet elderly man greeted us and warmly invited us in. It was a small, pleasantly furnished room, and what struck me was that in every free spot, tiny plastic figurines stood and sat—little toys. I told him why we had come. He received my indignation with understanding, but he indicated that because of the many thefts, they had been forced to introduce measures. Although he did not agree with the barred closures, he said, unfortunately he could do little. Still, he promised he would definitely deliver my complaint to the archbishop. Then we began to talk. Despite his advanced age, he was mentally remarkably fresh—well-informed, intelligent. It was a very pleasant experience, and an instructive one. I realized I must not let fear of the unknown prevent me from reaching my goals. I'm not claiming I personally made them reopen the churches to the public, but I do believe that when people raise their voices for aims they consider important, it truly has an effect, and consequences. I went home feeling good, satisfied.

Everyone has to face their own fears. For me, that had seemed like an insurmountable obstacle—and if my mentor hadn't been with me, I'm sure I would never have dared to ring that bell. The idea that I might stand up against an injustice, own my opinion, or hold someone accountable for something—that would have been unthinkable before. I imagined myself a tough girl, but in reality I was a timid little mouse.

That visit, though, began to strengthen my confidence. While my mentor is raising me, he never nags, never demands the impossible. He gives tasks through which the weaker side of my character can grow stronger. This visit was one of those. If I want to develop, I must test myself, and I must clear the obstacles as a winner. He always assigns tasks that press against the boundary of what I can do at that moment—without ever exceeding it. Like a good parent who brings out the best in a child—not with pointless praise, but by valuing performance. Though he very rarely praises anyone at all. I learned from him—and I got used to it—that before every action I examine my feelings. The right decision is always paired with a good feeling; the wrong one with a bad. He also taught me never to do anything out of routine. Everyone tends to respond to a given situation by habit. That is not right. You must always weigh it. He follows every aspect of my life, and by keeping his thoughtful advice, my chaotic, seemingly hopeless life took a one-hundred-eighty-degree turn. Not overnight. But today I can be proud of what I have achieved, of where I have arrived. My mentor's work as a mentor is not limited to wise advice and teaching. He has extraordinary abilities—astonishing and incomprehensible even to me—that make it possible for him to say, before certain events occur, what is going to happen. One such time was when we were on the road somewhere by car. I was driving, and well before a blind curve he told me to slow down, because a truck was coming toward us in our lane. I braked, and when we reached the curve I saw that an oncoming truck was passing illegally. It was able to finish the pass only because I was going slowly. If I had held my speed and not slowed down, it would have ended in a head-on collision. More than once we escaped an accident because he warned of the danger ahead of time.

One of the greatest tests of my life—the one my mentor confronted me with—was my trip to the Caribbean, and the stakes of that test were far more serious than I thought. I had to solve a long series of challenges in a highly intensified situation, often risking my physical safety, in order to complete the trial successfully. I had to prove to him that I deserved the energy he invested in me—that it was worth working with me—because I do not treat tasks lightly. Beyond that, it became clear to me as well: I am capable of everything. No obstacle can stop me. My determination has no boundaries. I received proof that I can overcome any difficulty, that my abilities far exceed the level I had previously imagined for myself. But I did not expect hardships like those. It was unimaginably hard—yet I cleared the obstacles with success.

This path is the most authentic proof of my mentor's angel-worthy, unexplainable ability. The chain of events matched, astonishingly, point by point, what he had outlined for me in detail months before departure—preparing me for it with the black humor so characteristic of him. He told me he had planned a trip where there would be no one who spoke our language. I am not a native English speaker, and I don't even speak English—this book, too, was originally written in my native language. I laughed, because I thought: there's no way there won't be at least one person from our country somewhere. He told me I would miss the plane, that I would be attacked, and that the plane would crash—here of course he was joking, but he explained that flying would not be trouble-free. Then he continued: my money would be taken. When full panic broke out in me, he also reassured me: don't worry, there will be an old man in a hat on the ship, and he will help me. From that point on, I would be able to enjoy the journey. Then, as a final jab, he added that there would still be one more twist at the end. The description of the man in the hat was concrete enough that I could recognize the help—but about the rest he gave no specifics, because, as he said, it would have been too much help. So throughout the whole trip I existed in high-alert mode, which was mentally exhausting. He did say it, but at the time I didn't yet fully grasp that every difficulty and every help that would roll into my path in that trial had been carefully and thoroughly organized in advance—just not in the way we humans organize things. For him it is completely normal that he arranged this journey on that level, in that depth. For me it was—and still is—utterly incomprehensible and unimaginable how he could execute it. And let's be honest: this is not normal. No human being could do this under any circumstances. For the human mind, it is impossible. How he does such things, and how they work—we do not know, and we will never know. No matter how we ask, he always says: don't even ask, because we cannot understand it, and he could not teach it to us. Not because he looks down on us, but because it is far beyond our abilities. Even today I cannot measure—let alone comprehend—this power of his that is unimaginable within earthly existence. I only know—and this is true for his other students as well—that most of the time our mouths literally hang open. His knowledge, his skill, his intelligence—how he functions, what he is—are that astonishing.

The Trial

In order to generate real changes in my life, to measure the strength and potential that lived inside me, and so that my mentor could convince himself of my suitability—of my abilities, endurance, steadfastness, resourcefulness—he placed me before a test that nearly brushed the edge of the impossible. He said I had to go very far away, to a place with no familiar ground under my feet, where I couldn't speak to anyone in my native language. Then I would find out what I was truly worth. The assignment was to choose an active, eventful itinerary—something like a cruise that touched multiple ports. I chose a Nile cruise, but he wouldn't even hear of it. He said there would be people there I could speak with in my own language, so it wasn't a challenge. He would choose for me. And he did. He came with me to the travel agency, where he selected a Caribbean luxury cruise.

Organized by a Spanish cruise line, Pullmantur. The flight would take us from

Madrid to Havana, where we would set sail on their ship, the *Zenith*. The route: Cuba, Mexico, Jamaica, the Cayman Islands, Cuba. The ship was two hundred yards long, fifty yards wide, and set out with sixteen hundred guests and a crew of six hundred eighty. An eight-day voyage, full board, a luxury suite. I was terrified. How was I supposed to get through this when I didn't speak any foreign language? In German I could—barely—say who I was and where I came from, but what was I going to do overseas with my little bit of German? In English, besides "yes" and "no," the only word I knew was "monkey." I knew even that only because George Michael had a song by that title, and it was one of my favorites. There were three months left until departure. I immediately enrolled in an English course, where three times a week for an hour and a half I tried to learn some basic vocabulary—or at least enough to read written text. It wasn't easy, and back then there were no mobile apps and no translation programs at my disposal— only the good old pocket dictionary. And I needed two of them, for translation in both directions, which stuffed my bag so full there was barely room for anything else. As part of my preparation, my mentor reminded me of the events he had already told me were waiting ahead. He set two conditions for the journey. I could not sit in my cabin, and I had to participate in every program I could. He always said that if you prepare for the worst, then anything that comes will be better than that. I followed his advice, fulfilled his conditions, and truly—everything happened exactly as he had "predicted."

On a beautiful day in March, I flew to Madrid. I was forty-six then, and I had never in my life traveled anywhere alone, and I had never been on an airplane. In that sense, too, I had to step out of my comfort zone, and that was no small thing. I tried to reduce my luggage to the minimum, because I didn't want to suffer all the way to the ship like a packhorse. Packing wasn't simple, because this was a luxury cruise where evening dinner required dressy attire. Men needed at least a suit and tie, women a cocktail dress or an evening gown. So I needed a large suitcase, a travel bag I could carry onto the plane, and a handbag as well. I enjoyed flying tremendously, and nothing went wrong—until we landed in Madrid. That's where the adventures began. The organized trip started on Saturday, when at 1:00 p.m. the plane would depart Madrid and take us to Havana, the ship's departure point. Since my own plane would have landed in Madrid at the same time—Saturday at 1:00 p.m.—the connection would have been impossible, so I had to go a day earlier. Back home, at the travel agency, I was told that on Friday a representative from the assigned hotel would be waiting at the airport with a sign, and would take me by bus to the company's five-star hotel, where I could stay at their expense. I thought: fine. So far, so good. The plane landed. I walked calmly toward the exit—and that's where I got my first shock. No one was waiting on the arrivals side.

Anyone who has been to the Madrid airport knows it's enormous. I stood there, waiting, thinking maybe someone would appear—nowhere, no one. Eventually I got tired of standing. Loaded down with my bags, I followed the people heading out, watching where they went. After getting lost several times, I finally found the bus station where the hotel shuttles were waiting, but unfortunately none of them was mine. By then every bus had left, and I had already been waiting an hour. After a while the drivers who were still there noticed me. They came over and asked questions, but since they spoke Spanish, I just kept repeating the hotel's name. They waved their hands, telling me to stay there; my bus would come. I waited another hour. Finally a bus appeared with my hotel's name on it. The relief was immense, because by then I was completely spent. I climbed aboard, and it took me straight to the hotel. I thought: at last I can relax, I can go to the restroom, eat, drink—because at the airport I hadn't dared to go anywhere, afraid I'd miss the bus. I marched up to the front desk with determination, handed over my passport and my reservation, and waited. And then the woman began explaining something and handed my papers back. I didn't understand what the problem was, and I didn't understand what the receptionist was saying. She tried several languages, but of course I understood none of them. Finally she pushed my papers toward me again and, not particularly kindly, motioned toward the door—outside was roomier. I stood there, baffled. What? I tried to grasp what she meant, and finally she showed me on the computer: my reservation wasn't in the system, so she couldn't give me a room. I should go somewhere else. That's when my fighting spirit flooded in. I pointed at my reservation and, using my meager English, asked, "Is this the hotel name?" Yes. "And on my reservation this hotel name is written?" Yes again. "Then what's the problem?" I asked. In her view, the problem was that I wasn't in the system, so they wouldn't give me a room, and I should leave. I indicated I didn't care. Give me a room, or I'm sleeping here in the lobby. She tried to usher me out, but I dug in. I set my things down on the couch opposite her and began staring at her with an annoyed, unblinking gaze. I drove her crazy. Finally she made a couple of phone calls—and lo and behold, five hours after arriving in Madrid, I got a room. Keycard in hand: eighth floor. I reach the door, try to open it—nothing. No matter what I did, it wouldn't work. My nerves were completely depleted. I couldn't believe this was real. The thought of hauling all my luggage back down to the front desk to explain the problem with hands and feet—it would have taken more strength than I had. I nearly burst into tears, but in the end I pulled myself together. It occurred to me that in a hotel this big, there had to be housekeeping on every floor—someone with keys to every room—and surely someone was nearby. I continued the thought. Since housekeeping likely wasn't Spanish but some kind of immigrant, maybe they would be more understanding. I hoped it would be easier to communicate, because perhaps they didn't speak Spanish either, and I could show them what was wrong. I put my suitcase and bag down by the door and went exploring. I listened for the sounds of cleaning, or looked for dirty linens left in the hallway. The hotel was L-shaped, so I didn't have to go far; around the corner I suddenly heard the hum of a vacuum. I knocked, and I was right. I ran into a cleaning woman who spoke a Slavic language. I exchanged my bad key for a working one, and at last—victorious—I got into my room. I unpacked, exhaled, refreshed myself, then went down to dinner. Afterward I climbed into bed immediately. No rocking required—I slept like a stone. The next morning I woke early. Since my flight left at 1:00 p.m., I decided to use the time I had and take a morning sightseeing trip. Still, to cover every possibility, I would go to the airport two hours early, because given how this trip had begun, anything could happen.

I wanted to prevent trouble. I believed I had prepared wisely for potential problems. My hotel was in a new district, among newly built office buildings of global corporations, surrounded by a huge park, next to sports facilities. At 7:30 a.m. I went down to the front desk. Using my limited English to the very edge of its capacity, I asked what I should see in such a short time. They were very helpful: they gave me a map and marked the main sights and the metro lines, including where I should get off. The metro stop wasn't close— about half a mile on foot—but it looked like a pleasant walk. I went down into the underpass and tried to buy a ticket, but they couldn't make change, and the card reader was broken. Since nothing in the area was open where I could get change, I had to go back to the hotel. So the problems began again. I changed money at the desk, walked back to the metro booth, and finally got a ticket. I validated it. I had just passed through the gate when I realized I'd left my map in the ticket window. I tried to go back, but the barrier wouldn't let me. I was about to climb over when I saw the armed soldier standing watch at the entrance lift his weapon from his shoulder and aim it at me. My blood turned cold. It hit me then that not long before, there had been a terrorist attack in Madrid, and heightened security was in effect. I raised my hands immediately and started pointing toward the booth, chanting "Karte, karte!"—hoping he might understand German. The poor man stared at me blankly, trying to figure out what on earth I wanted, but seeing I was only a crazed tourist, he lowered his weapon and let me climb back for the map. It's not an everyday experience to have a loaded weapon pointed at you. I had been afraid I would get lost in the metro, but the system is plastered with such practical, logical signs that it's almost impossible to lose your way. I got off at the marked station, went up to street level, and blended into the tourist crowd. I love architecture, so with my camera in my hand I couldn't take my eyes off the arches and façades. I was enchanted.

As I wandered the streets, suddenly a terrible feeling rose in me. My bag was on my right shoulder, and in that hand I also held the camera, raised high because I was looking upward, filming the façades. Without moving my arm, I lowered only my head and glanced at my bag. I nearly screamed. A man's hand was under the flap, trying to open the zipper. Out of the corner of my eye I registered there were three of them. Two hard-looking men had boxed me in, with a woman in the middle shielding them. In a split second I had to decide what to do. I didn't want to shout, because then they would rip the bag off my shoulder, shove me down, and run. No one would have understood what I was shouting anyway. I couldn't expect help. People react slowly in such situations; by the time they realized what was happening, my attackers would be long gone. They terrified me. All my money, my passport, my room key—everything precious—was in that bag. I had to decide in a millisecond. I didn't want to give them an opening by speaking a foreign language. I knew I needed the shock effect—but without revealing

I wasn't Spanish. In the end I gathered every scrap of nerve, turned to face them, gestured with my hand, and barked at them with a furious "AHHH!"—which, of course, means the same thing in every language. They looked at me, startled, but I returned their stare with fierce determination. This was not what they had expected. They didn't quite know what to do with it, and they slipped away quickly. I had gained a little time to collect myself. Years ago my shop had been broken into more than once, and when we noticed it quickly, the burglars couldn't finish what they came for. The police who arrived afterward told us: if the burglars don't complete their job, they often come back, and they'll be lurking nearby to see whether the coast is clear. That time they caught the man within an hour; he was waiting not far from my shop, and they even found the few stolen items on him. The officer's words came back to me immediately. I knew I wasn't safe yet. With shaking hands I checked my things; fortunately nothing was missing. I was certain they were watching somewhere, waiting for the right moment. I didn't move. Instead I began watching people methodically— and since an alley opened from that street every fifty yards or so, it was perfect terrain for pickpockets. And then I saw them: all three of them, lurking at the corner of the nearest alley. But by then I knew what I was going to do. I took out my phone and started typing a number that didn't exist. My phone began telling me that the number did not exist. My attackers didn't know that, so the trick worked perfectly. They were far enough away that they couldn't hear what I was saying, but close enough to see what I was doing, so I pretended someone had answered. I moved like someone dictating an address. I looked up above the building entrances; I even walked a little farther because the one I'd been standing in front of didn't have a number. With an Italian temperament I performed indignation into my deaf phone, all the while looking at the criminals and pointing them out. When I finished the performance, I looked at them and ended the call with a theatrical gesture. Their expressions said it all: they had swallowed it. As a final flourish, with raised eyebrows I pointed at them threateningly, then put my hands on my hips and acted as if I were waiting for someone. They visibly panicked. They shook their fists at me, but they didn't come closer—they fled through the alley. That day I did a service for law enforcement and for the unsuspecting tourists, because I'm sure that gang didn't dare return to that hunting ground for quite a while.

But I had had enough of sightseeing. My hands and legs were trembling. I decided I'd rather wait for departure in my hotel room. I didn't want any more excitement. I didn't know it wouldn't be the last of it that day. After I got back to the hotel, and after a short rest, since I still had time, I took a pleasant walk in the hotel park. Then I brought my suitcase and travel bag down to the front desk. The travel agency had specifically emphasized that when I left the hotel, I wasn't supposed to carry my suitcase; I should leave it at the desk, they would attach the identification tag and take it out to the airport. With that certainty and great confidence, I brought my luggage down. For this occasion I had even memorized the question in English, and I carried my dictionary too, just in case—so there wouldn't be any misunderstanding. I asked the clerk, "Will you take my luggage to the airport?" "Yes," he answered. "So I don't have to take it?" I asked again. "No, we take it," he repeated. "Are you sure?" I pressed, confused. I even showed him the word in my dictionary. By then he looked at me as if I were insane, but he nodded yes. All right, then. I thought everything was settled, and I handed over my suitcase. He put on the paper strip and locked the bags in a storage room. I found it odd that he put them there, but since he insisted they would take them, fine—this must be how it's done. Someone responsible would come and collect them.

I said goodbye and boarded the bus that took us to the airport. I did what I had planned the day before and truly went out to the airport two hours before departure. I thought I'd check in and then wait in the lounge so I wouldn't miss the flight. I waited through an unbearably long line. When I reached the counter, I handed the woman my passport and boarding pass. She looked at me, astonished, and asked: "Where is your suitcase?" I said the hotel would bring it. She looked even more surprised, but she could tell she was dealing with a beginner, so in a calm, slow voice she explained that I could only check in with my suitcase. She couldn't let me proceed. Well, this was lovely. I thanked her for the information and blessed my own prudence for coming early—at least this wasn't discovered at the last minute. I wasn't panicking yet. I thought there was still time. I believed the hotel shuttle ran every half hour. I thought I was still just in time. I would go to the bus stop, tell the driver to bring my suitcase on the next run, and I'd be fine. Not a bad plan— except the bus didn't come, and I had an hour left until the plane departed. That's when sweat broke out on me. I couldn't wait any longer. I went to the information desk and asked the woman to look up my hotel's phone number. I wanted to call and tell them to bring my luggage immediately. The information clerk asked: "B&B Hotel Madrid?" I said yes. She asked, utterly calmly, "Which one? Because there are two five-star hotels in Madrid with that name." I nearly fainted. How could that be? Two five-star hotels with the same name in the same city? It was incomprehensible. My mind couldn't accept that they could be so unimaginative that they couldn't come up with a new name for a hotel. But my indignation didn't change reality. Her final question delivered the finishing blow. She asked which district the hotel was in, because if I could tell her, she could identify it and give me the phone number. Oh. Now I was truly in trouble. I had no idea. Who remembers something like that? I thanked her—though it didn't help me much—and walked away.

My cell phone couldn't use the Spanish network, because back home I'd forgotten to activate roaming with the phone company. And at the airport there were special coin-operated wall phones, with five or six people waiting in front of them. And as if that weren't enough, you had to buy the phone coins in a shop. The shop line was so long I would have grown a white beard before it was my turn. And even if I had managed to call, how would I have made myself understood? In what language? So my situation became critical. Only one solution remained. I ran out to the taxi stand, jumped into a taxi, and told the Spanish-speaking driver only one thing: "GO!" He tried to ask where to "Go!", but I just waved both hands and kept repeating, "Go, go!" Then I pointed to my eyes with two fingers and pointed into the distance—meaning: I'll navigate by gestures; you just drive, and fast. Every nerve in my body went taut. He didn't ask again. He floored it. I knew the hotel was only about twenty minutes from the airport—but it would take as long to get back. And then I still had to find my airline's counter and check in. Not a simple equation when you have less than an hour for everything. It was a miracle that I—who gets lost everywhere—was able to guide the taxi back to the hotel. I owe that to my love of architecture, because on my first ride toward the hotel I had seen such striking new buildings that I remembered the route by them. When we finally stopped at the hotel, I sprinted to the front desk. Needless to say, my suitcases were still in the storage room. By then I wasn't even surprised. I spoke to the receptionist, grabbed my things, jumped back into the taxi, and urged the driver to take me back to the airport. I had almost no time left. I checked in at a run and sprinted to the gate. Two minutes to departure. I ran to the plane. When I finally reached it and boarded, they were already closing the door. I had barely sat down when the plane began to move. They were waiting for me. Most likely my first attempt to check in without a suitcase had left a strong impression on the woman at the counter, and she told them to wait because an inexperienced woman had gone back for her luggage. Later, when I had time to think it through, I realized the hotel staff really would have taken my suitcases out to the airport—together with me. But no one had told me, an inexperienced beginner, that in such situations I and my luggage are one inseparable unit. In other words, it was obvious to them that they would take my suitcase to the airport with me. But I was already at the airport, so the hotel staff found only the suitcases, not me. Exhausted, drained, I sat in my seat and thought: My God—if it starts like this, what else is waiting for me?

At first, the flight calmed me. Until we reached the Atlantic, nothing notable happened. But once we were over the water, my mentor's "prophecy" caught up with me again. We hit turbulence so strong the plane started bucking and tossing, and the flight attendants hurried through the cabin pulling down every window shade. The seatbelt sign came on, and everyone had to buckle up. We held our cups in our hands, otherwise everything would have sloshed out. Even so, later we were cleaning up what hadn't stayed inside them. It wasn't pleasant to see the frightened face of the stewardess sitting almost across from me—even though she tried to hide it. All anyone could do was hope nothing serious would happen to the aircraft. The plane shook and jumped. Strange noises came from it. It was frightening, that's certain. Thank God, twenty minutes later it ended. After eleven hours we arrived safely in Havana. On that plane only the passengers of that luxury ship were traveling—the same ship I had a ticket for. After I got off, I still had to find my luggage. The seasoned, sharp-eyed travelers immediately pressed toward the conveyor. Every group has people who insist on being first at everything, always. They wanted to step onto the ship first, too. The buses waited in a line at the exit. As soon as one filled up, it departed. The crowd thinned steadily, but my suitcase simply wouldn't appear on the belt. Another stress point. I began to see horrors. I was sure my luggage had been put on another plane, and I would have to live through the whole week in whatever I was wearing. Everyone had boarded the bus except for five people whose luggage hadn't arrived. Naturally, I was one of the five. Luckily the other four were German. One of them spoke English well, so he investigated. Since I understand German better, I learned from them what was going on. As it turned out, we weren't supposed to carry our luggage at all—it would be waiting for us at the door of our cabins. So that's how I learned that not only had I not needed to haul my things from the hotel to the airport, I didn't need to haul them from the airport to the ship either. How much anxiety that knowledge would have spared me, if I'd had it in time.

At last I reached the port. When I stepped off the bus, the ship towered in front of me. Anyone who has seen an ocean liner knows. And anyone who hasn't—can't imagine how enormous these things can be. I stood there amazed. I knew the dimensions, I'd seen pictures, but seeing it with my own eyes was something else entirely. I have to admit: they did everything properly. We boarded between rows of crew in white sailor uniforms, and they welcomed us ceremonially. The interior was dreamlike. I can only speak in superlatives. In the lobby they took everyone's small and large bags away. Then each female passenger was escorted to her cabin arm-in-arm by a sailor in a white uniform. I got an escort with a charming smile. When I was alone in my cabin, I looked around. A balcony with a sea view, a fruit bowl on the table, water set out, a gift backpack, and other gift items placed on the bed. It was wonderful. Soon there was a knock. A young woman handed me some papers. One was the check-in form, which I had to fill out and submit at the reception. Since cash couldn't be used for payment during the whole trip, the rules stated that a certain amount would be pre-authorized on an accepted bank card. I had already seen the list of acceptable card types at the travel agency. If necessary, however, you could also leave a cash deposit at the ship's cashier. Because we had checked in the agency that my card met the requirements, I wasn't worried. I also had some dollars in cash, in case I wanted to buy something in port. So I took the form down. About an hour later, there was a knock. The same woman stood at the door. From her words I gathered there was a problem, and I should go to reception. I wasn't even surprised. I was sick of it. What now—again? I went down. The receptionist said there was a small problem. The problem was that the system would not accept my bank card. I tried to make her understand that was impossible. I had seen the list myself at the agency; she must have missed it. She hadn't missed it. I should look at her monitor. She turned it toward me and indeed: my card type wasn't listed. No matter how much money I had on that card, I couldn't use it. She explained that either I put down the required amount as a deposit, or I had to get off the ship and could not take part in the trip. Perfect. What else could possibly come next? In the end I paid the deposit in cash—but that meant all of it. I had only a few dollars left to buy anything in port. After that I didn't dare consume anything extra on the ship either, because I definitely wanted to participate in the excursions, and I didn't know exactly how much those would cost. It wasn't pleasant. In fact I can say it was humiliating. Luckily it was early spring, not too hot yet, so I didn't crave a lot of liquids. Back then I drank very little—less than average, even. So the main thing was: I could stay, and the ship departed.

The stress had wrecked me, and it still wasn't over. Because I couldn't communicate properly with anyone, I didn't know where anything was on the ship. Every day we received a bulletin about the next day's programs, but I couldn't understand a single word. So every evening after dinner I sat down until midnight and looked up the entire thing in the dictionary so I'd have some idea what was happening on the ship. Even though they announced everything over the loudspeaker in five languages, they spoke so quickly that I understood nothing at all. My only help was my cabin stewardess, who spoke slowly—so that with my dictionary I could translate—and told me what I wanted to know, or what she wanted to warn me about. She said if there was trouble I should just shout her name; she was on my deck and would come help. I was very grateful. On a ship like that, the crew works an insane amount; they barely sleep, and yet they never showed fatigue or bad mood. They were charming and kind from the first day to the last, transforming the week into something beautiful for us. We traveled by ship at night, and in the mornings we anchored in a new country's harbor. If we went ashore, everyone could join one of the programs they had chosen, or explore on their own. Or we could stay on the ship, because countless activities and games entertained the passengers. My cabin was elegant and large. With my own stewardess, who moved like an invisible fairy: I saw her only if I wanted to, but I always felt her presence. Whenever I went to the bathroom and dried my hands on the towel, it seemed that by the time I noticed, she had already replaced it. The corner of the toilet paper roll's last sheet was folded into a triangle after every use. In the evening after dinner, when I returned to my cabin, the upper right corner of my blanket was turned down, and my nightgown was laid out fan-shaped in the middle of the bed. The care and attention felt good to my shaken soul. My nerves were so exhausted from constant tension that I wanted nothing more than to crawl under the covers and not set foot outside my cabin until the end of the week. I was so overwhelmed that one evening I had a sobbing fit. I cried for hours in my bed. I could barely stop.

But I couldn't hide. I had come on this journey because I wanted to prove—to myself—that the insults that had followed me through my life were not true. I am not the helpless loser my husband made me out to be, the woman who can't even pay a bill. And I never forgot, even for a moment during the trip, that when I got home my mentor would hold me strictly accountable for my actions. I knew I had to show him that I could develop, that I was worthy of his effort. I had always thought of myself as a tough, daring, independent, strong woman who could survive on an ice floe. But somewhere in the thick of life, that got lost. Here I could prove it to myself. I knew I would regret it bitterly if I ran. When I had cried myself out, I gathered every ounce of strength and courage and made a battle plan. I planned how I would manage. First, because the ship was enormous and I didn't want to get lost, I constantly peeked out my door and watched where people went, then followed them. At first I didn't go far—only as far as I could still find my way back. My first distant goal was to find the restaurant where dinner was served. I went after the others—a tactic that worked for me throughout the entire voyage. Dinner service happened in two seatings. I was in the second. In the restaurant I realized that on the entire ship I was the only person traveling alone. Friend groups, families, couples—no one was alone except me. And as if that weren't enough, among neither guests nor crew was there a single person who spoke my language. As it later turned out, this was unusual, because normally there are always at least a few of my compatriots—either among the guests or among the crew. There were some on the previous cruise, and there would be some on the next. I had prepared myself for this in advance, because I knew it would happen. My dear, mischievous mentor had told me, and planned it. Still, experiencing it wasn't easy. So I went into the restaurant, which was nearly full—more than three hundred people. You can imagine. Naturally every pair of eyes turned toward me when, in the middle of that massive dining room, I was led to a table for one. The staff's attentiveness and professionalism showed in the fact that one waiter stayed beside my table for the entire dinner service, so I didn't feel uncomfortable at all. He helped me sit, poured me water, and with a constant smile asked whether everything was all right, whether I was sure I felt fine. The others received excellent service too, but there one waiter served four tables, running back and forth, hardly able to offer such personalized attention or to chat with guests. They must have thought I was some very important person, if I was being fussed over like that.

After I had translated the program bulletin in the evenings, I chose which activities I wanted. There were countless shows on the ship, and I tried to choose ones that didn't require language. So I learned juggling, I learned dancing, and I even took part in team games where we had an incredible time. I began to loosen up, and the crew seized every moment to check that I was all right. Then came the first shore excursion: Mexico. We could choose from several programs. I wanted to swim with dolphins. Besides me, nine others chose it. A hydrofoil carried us ashore. It was obvious they were a group. I sat a little apart. Suddenly one of the women turned to me and asked in English, "Where are you from?" I told her. She turned and interpreted it for the others. They responded with a big cheer, because it turned out the woman came from a country neighboring mine. She had come on the trip with her husband, an Italian coworker, that man's family, and their circle of friends. I learned that almost all of them were lawyers. Only the Italian family's grandfather was an architect, and the woman in the friend couple was a homemaker. They asked who I had come with. When they learned I was completely alone—and that I didn't speak foreign languages, or only very poorly—they were horrified. They immediately took me under their wing and insisted I stay with them. They were very kind, and they behaved like a true Italian family: speaking loudly, gesturing with wide arm movements. That kind of behavior isn't foreign to me either, but it was an interesting experience to watch them. Our hydrofoil reached shore late, so we should have hurried to the dolphinarium, but the Italian grandfather couldn't keep up. With aching legs, he could walk only with a cane. His family galloped ahead, stopping now and then to wave, calling out loudly for the old man to hurry. Poor man—no matter how he tried, he couldn't catch them. For a while I trotted at the front with the others because I was terrified of getting lost. But from time to time I fell back so the grandfather could reach at least within sight. Then I began worrying what would happen to him, because those young people just kept going—he would never catch up. In the end he'd get lost, and that was something I would not have been able to live with. So, whatever happens, I stayed with him. I thought I would come up with something if we got into trouble. There we were, the two of us, walking along the road, trying to communicate. But since he spoke only Italian, and I didn't speak a single word of it, it was difficult—yet by pointing and gesturing we understood each other. I found it sweet that he kept speaking Italian to me while I kept repeating in my own language that I didn't understand. And still he went on and on. Anyone who saw us would have thought we were having a wonderful conversation. I felt he was very grateful that I stayed with him. Soon he introduced himself. His name was Angelo. And then came the most important—and most astonishing—event. Until then the weather had been gloomy, but suddenly the sun came out, and it became very warm. Angelo reached into his backpack, and—like a miracle—took out his hat and put it on his head.

I was stunned. There in front of me stood the man in the hat my mentor had "predicted." He matched the description perfectly. And of course his name—what else could it be—was Angelo, which means angel. Another proof. Later we caught up with the others, and we hadn't missed anything, because no matter how we rushed, we still couldn't have participated in the group swim. That day's slots had filled much earlier. Still, we had a lovely day. We rested, swam, sunbathed, bought gifts. Late afternoon we returned to the ship.

Soon it was time for dinner. I had just taken my royal seat when someone behind me called my name. I turned around, and—what can I say—Angelo and his group were sitting at the table behind mine. It turned out we were in the same dining group. This could not be coincidence. They expressed their boundless goodwill and generosity by inviting me to their table. They even arranged it with the waiter, so my place setting and chair were moved. From then until the end of the trip we ate dinner together, and they even paid for my water. They would have paid for more, but I don't drink alcohol, and I absolutely didn't want to be a burden. It honored me that they considered me part of their company. From that point on, I spent almost every moment with Angelo and the Italian couple who were friends with the group. They were closer to me in age. The younger ones with the children liked busier entertainment than we did, but I think they were glad the grandfather had found companionship. We ate breakfast together in the mornings, and after a while—however unbelievable it sounds—we understood each other's words. The four of us became so attuned that language no longer posed an obstacle; it was as if we were conversing telepathically. It was incredible—not only to me, but to those around us. People stopped at our table in astonishment, trying to decipher our conversation, or guess what language we were speaking. Italian they could recognize, perhaps, but I doubt they could identify my native language. They looked at us strangely when the three of them spoke Italian to me and I answered in my own language. And it wasn't a simple question-and-answer exchange; they told funny stories about things that had happened to them on the trip. Amazingly, I understood everything, and they understood me, and all the while we laughed until we could hardly breathe. After that, at every port we chose the same excursions. In the evenings we went to shows together, soaked in the hot tub, or swam in one of the ship's pools.

We found one another, truly, and I enjoyed every minute, so the remainder of the trip passed pleasantly. At last the stressful moments stopped. Just as my mentor's "prophecy" had said.

The moment of farewell arrived. The trip ended, and everyone was heading home. I managed my money well, so I participated in every program I wanted. There was enough for the necessary expenses, too. By the end there wasn't a cent left from the deposit, but I thought: I won't need anything now anyway; we're leaving Cuba soon. My plane ticket is secured. In Madrid I'll be able to use my bank card again and the problem will be solved. So I went to the airport calmly. I got in line. Passport control was just beginning when a low grumbling spread. As it turned out, everyone who wanted to leave Cuba had to pay five U.S. dollars. If you didn't pay, they wouldn't let you board the plane. My blood went cold. I didn't have a penny. And here I still couldn't pay with my bank card. The twist my mentor had promised—right before the end. I began to panic. If I couldn't pay, I would have to stay. And that was the last thing I wanted. Angelo saw my desperation. He asked what was wrong. I felt terribly embarrassed, but I told him. He took out his wallet—stuffed with money—and held it out. He said I should take as much as I wanted. It was an unbelievably generous offer. I took no more than five dollars, and I showed him. I thanked him and said I would transfer the money to him as soon as I got home. He waved it off. It didn't matter, he said—this wasn't money. But it mattered to me. I didn't want to remain in his debt. As we stood in line, the ship's activities coordinator appeared and asked for a moment of attention. She explained that because of the storm we hadn't been able to dock in the Cayman Islands, so passengers who couldn't use the planned program there were entitled to a refund. She called passengers by name. Including mine. When I stepped forward, she pressed the money into my hand. And how much was it? Five dollars. Fate—or my incredible mentor—who knows? Let everyone decide for themselves. In any case, one of them is a funny but very powerful player, that much must be admitted. Of course I immediately returned Angelo's money. We both smiled. On the plane we all left Cuba safely. When we arrived in Madrid and it was time to say goodbye, he invited me to his summer house in Italy—to spend a week with them, if I wanted. I accepted with joy, and the following summer I did visit them, and they received me with such kindness and warmth—but that is another story. I kept in touch with him for a long time, and then one day he simply stopped answering. I knew he was preparing for surgery. Since he was very old, I believe death separated us, but I will keep his memory in my heart always, and my gratitude to his family.

After I came home, my first stop was my mentor. I told him everything in detail. His first reaction was to laugh at me, and then he said everything had happened exactly as he had planned. I don't know how he does it, but over the years there were many times when he described future events in advance—how they would happen, and when. When I asked how he could "predict" so precisely, he answered that he was not a fortune-teller and he did not predict anything. He had planned my Caribbean trip in detail and ensured that everything happened exactly that way. And to the question of how— his answer was always the same: I didn't need to know everything, and in any case I wouldn't be able to comprehend or interpret the "how" of it. By now I understand he doesn't say this because he thinks I'm stupid. That is not like him at all. He says it because it is truly so. He reassured me that I had completed the trial successfully, and I had even earned one of his exceedingly rare praises. I feel that this was when I won his trust. That trust is worth more to me than any compliment. Throughout the entire trip, my task was to carry out the assigned challenges, proving my aptitude and that I was worthy of trust. I could have failed easily. But it lifted my self-worth enormously that I didn't run. I didn't back down. I mobilized even the last crumbs of my reserves—and met the challenge. This journey left an extraordinarily deep mark on me. Since then, whenever I face difficulty, I can always draw strength from this experience. I am proud that although my unknowable mentor has put many people to the test, I belong to the few who did not fail.

Growth

My mentor teaches that the vast majority of people are incapable of change on their own—they need outside help. I belong to that majority. I have my own struggles, and the greatest battles I must fight are with myself. However much I once imagined that I was already such a good person I could teach others—I was wrong. Today I see clearly: I had, and still have, plenty of room to grow. Before I met my Angel mentor, I found no answers—none beyond doubt—to the questions that occupied me. Only through him did I receive them. He invested immense work in my development. He set, and still sets, a high standard before me. Behind his strict accountability there is always care, and that gave me—and still gives me—a deep sense of security. Before I came to know him, I lived the ordinary life of ordinary people, and worked an enormous amount besides. Job, cooking, ironing, studying with the child, watching television, an occasional party with so-called friends who again and again prove they are not really your friends. Yet you don't want to lose them, because you're afraid that then you'll truly lose contact with everyone. Now and then a long weekend without the child, and once a year a shared weeklong vacation by the sea. The only connection with your partner is arguing; otherwise life passes in boredom and tension, slowly consuming you. You come home from work, eat, sit down in front of the TV with a beer in your hand—or a tray of pastries—then go to sleep. The next day everything begins again. There is nothing wrong with that, if it is enough for someone. Who decides for you what is good for you? No one. It is your life—if it feels right to you, live it. For me it was not enough. Yet I did nothing—only rebelled, instead of acting with resolve. And yet the possibility is always there. The question is whether we dare to live with that possibility. I did not dare to risk what would happen if I spoke up about my desires, my ideas. I am an intensely curious person, and I love learning. Not what and not the way they teach in school, but what I can gain experience from. I was astonishingly ignorant in every area. When I might have begun to change, I was so arrogant, so self-satisfied, so egoistic that I swept every offered solution or opportunity off the table if it didn't come from someone flattering me. I chose the easier path: deflecting responsibility. I believed I was not the cause of the situation—I was only the victim. But that leads nowhere, because everyone who comes into contact with me thinks the same about themselves. And so begins the pointing of fingers, the blaming of one another. A stream of complaints without end, with not the smallest sign of seeking a solution. Thanks to my mentor, I grew up. At forty-six I had my first computer, which I received from him so I could carry out the tasks he entrusted to me. Until then I didn't even know how to turn one on or how it worked. But I had to become capable, so I forced myself to learn. Today I can use it at a user level without difficulty.

I love music. And in this, too, he opened a new world for me. We often listen to music together, and I gained a great deal of new knowledge that way. My musical taste developed and refined through him. Before, I consumed everything indiscriminately, but thanks to him I now value quality over quantity—and not only in music. I deeply enjoy being able to devote time to meaningful pursuits, including listening to music. Now that I have learned music develops intelligence, I can only recommend it to everyone. Not as background noise, but with attention and feeling. It can pluck strings in the human soul you never even knew were there. Before I met him, I didn't even know I had possibilities. I didn't know I could achieve anything, realize anything, reach my desires if I worked for them. Through my development I learned how to live—and how not to abuse my opportunities. Thanks to my mentor's inspiring guidance, I became capable of bringing many of them into reality. There were countless things I tried for the first time because of him. The atmosphere of these experiences awakened important feelings about life—and even more important inner growth. I chose the path of development, and I had to face the fact that there would be losses. I knew my environment would struggle to tolerate that I was beginning to grow up. They would never recognize or acknowledge how much I had changed for the better, because for them it meant losing control over me. I knew some relationships would deteriorate for this reason: they would notice that the easily directed, easily manipulated person I had been was disappearing, and they could not accept it. At such times aggression appears, and things can escalate even to abuse.

There were many instances of physical violence in my past. I condemned it then, and I condemn it now. Let anyone think what they will—violence is not acceptable in a relationship. In my new life, through my development, I embraced the understanding that it is unacceptable for someone to push another into servitude simply to rule over them. Only the weak, the base, and the foolish resort to violence—whether against a partner or against their children. I would be curious whether such an abuser would allow their boss to slap them for mistakes. Certainly not. Then how dare that person strike their own child for an error? Through my mentor I came to know a kind of freedom in which I could never again accept being a man's servant to the degree that so many women unfortunately are. This does not mean I exclude the possibility of finding a partner who, guided by similar principles, can live with me as an absolutely equal companion in freedom. I do have an example before me—once again, my Angel mentor. Perhaps it sounds repetitive, but it is true. His attitude toward people is completely different from the usual. For him there are no superior or subordinate roles; there is only equality. He has no demands of anyone, because, as he says, this is not important for him—it is important for us, for every human being. He resolves conflicts through constructive dialogue. Goodwill, the desire to help, and deep love make his relationships function flawlessly. In his own partnership—he has one, with four children—his wife does not live under oppression and can rely on him in everything. Their relationship is truly equal and partner-based. She is not restricted in anything, for my mentor believes his partner is not his property, not his servant, but an independent human being. An Angel treats his wife, his children, and everyone else as independent, free individuals. How wonderful it would have been to be born into such a family. Still, fate gave me the chance to make up for everything.

I feel I thought everything through carefully and did all that was necessary to make the best decision of my life when I chose the path my mentor offered. Through it I became a balanced, optimistic person, aware of my faults as well as my strengths—someone who stands by her principles with optimism and commitment. Following these principles brought me peace and freedom. At present I feel perfectly well alone, though I do not rule out that I may one day have a relationship again. If the time comes and I find someone who lives by the same principles as I do, I will step into it boldly and with confidence. Of course there were casual relationships whose purpose was simply to spend free time pleasantly, but none left a deep mark. A few years ago there was one connection—brief—that held the possibility of serious commitment. I was entirely content with being alone. Then fate—though based on the experiences of my past many years I would rather see my mentor's intervention in it—thought otherwise. After sixteen years alone, I received the great gift of my life in the person of a former high school classmate. He reached out to me through social media, and a personal meeting followed. In high school he had been very shy and withdrawn, but I had always considered him an infinitely kind and decent boy, so I invited him over. The possibility of meeting again made me curious. Although we both attended our five-year class reunions, we had never exchanged a word. We had impressions of one another, but we didn't truly know each other. He knew a few things about me; I knew nothing about him. It was the first time we spoke about deep matters—first in our lives. The planned brief, polite visit became hours of intimate conversation. I enjoyed every minute, and I listened with surprise as he told me that in high school he had harbored tender feelings for me. Knowing who I was back then, he would have had no chance with me—not because of him, but because my personality at that time was incapable of receiving such feelings. The quality of our meeting created the foundation for this openness to fall on fertile ground. Through our honest conversation I realized that long ago, when I yearned for a partner, this was exactly the type I had been searching for. Back then I did not believe I could ever have such a man—a calm, cheerful, attentive person who would regard me as an equal partner. For both of us it was a joyful rediscovery. Our first meeting was followed by others. Of all the relationships I had after my divorce, this one was the longest, the happiest, the most harmonious. I reveled in the expressions of love we discovered together.

And yet, after a while, I could not live this state fully, could not enjoy it without reservation. Indirectly it was caused by my more than twenty-year inner transformation, because I had to realize that the path I was on was more important to me than anything else. Although my mentor offered every support so that my relationship could work, a serious inner conflict slowly formed within me. I felt I had no choice but to end it, because I was becoming physically ill. I had to examine myself. What did I want more—a relationship, or to continue the path I had begun? Because if it was the second, I could not expose him to such a situation. It would have been unfair. I understood that the two things, unfortunately, could not function at the same time. My physical and psychological symptoms clearly signaled what I needed. Though the possibility of a relationship was very tempting, the energy I had invested in self-development for more than two decades—and the results I had achieved—were more important to me than anything. It was a difficult decision. The breakup devastated us both. But I am glad I recognized in time what I truly wanted and was able to take the step I needed. Before, I would never have been capable of that.

I advise everyone: do not be afraid to get to know yourself. It was only by facing myself—terrifying at first—that I could become the person I am now. The person I had always wanted to be. Someone worthy, at least in part, of the many qualities I once used to describe myself. If, back then, I had not been driven by the desire to change and truly become the person I imagined myself to be, I could never have experienced that relationship either. When I look back at the time before my suicide attempt, and I compare the person I was then with the person I became after decades supported by my mentor, only then is the immeasurable growth visible. The knowledge of how much I have grown makes me happy. For that reason I would not exchange my fate for anyone else's. I am grateful for every small success and every trial that demanded everything of me and led me here. Of course I do not believe this path is for everyone. Fulfillment is unique for each individual. I wish you, dear reader, that you may find the important milestones of your life and fight for your goals. Work for them, and your dream will come true. No matter how old you are, never say it is too late. It is never too late. Never give up on yourself, and you will receive what you have longed for. And perhaps—if you truly want it—you too will find your Angel. I give thanks to God that I may experience this personally, and I trust that fate will give me the chance to repay it with my life, with all the knowledge and effort I am capable of giving.

Catching Sight of God

I am among those whom religions repel—religions that suffocate the freedom of pure faith. I have never been able to accept the churches' dogmatic approach. And because the other option—most branches of esotericism—denies the concept of a God who stands above everything and everyone, they could not bring me any closer to spiritual being, either. For a long time I could not find a path that fit me. By the grace of my fate, I found an Angel—one who took me under his wing and became my mentor. The path he offered finally made it possible for even my boldest dream to come true. I was given a chance, with my own eyes, my own skin, my own senses—with my body and my soul, while still alive—to see God. I know. This is the extreme end of incredible things, and for many religious people it is taboo. And yet it is true. After fifteen years of persistent work and continuous growth, my mentor judged the time had come for me to live through something that goes far beyond any experience available to human beings. He saw that I had made the virtue of humility my own. Make no mistake: I am not speaking of humiliation, but humility. In the past I would have confused the two, but I have learned the difference. If I hold something—or someone—in great esteem, I recognize and acknowledge that this thing or person is, in some way, greater than I am. If that is so, respect is born in me. Which means I should not expect the thing or person I esteem to grant me that respect in advance. I must be the first to give the respect that is due, because that thing or person has already earned it by everything that makes me esteem them. That is humility. The fact that I was already doing well in humility was only the foundation. I also needed preparation—multi-step, special spiritual exercises. That was required for my mind to become capable of reaching and receiving what awaited me. One of the most frightening—and at the same time the most wondrous, the most extraordinary—experiences of my life. I caught sight of God. It truly was only a glimpse, because I would have been incapable of holding what I saw, what I felt, for any longer. This is not really only about seeing—though it is that too—but far more about perceiving with your whole being. With every cell, every current of energy, with your mind and your heart. And of course, with your soul. It is unbearably moving—and at the same time deeply shattering. I cannot reveal exactly how it happened. But I will share what I can.

It was night. Under the open sky, I lay on my back on the ground. I stared at the star-filled vault above me while my mentor gave instructions—what I had to do. Using the technique I had learned during my preparation, I tried to bring my mind, my soul, and my body—my entire being—into the proper state. Minutes passed, and I kept watching the universe above me, following the Angel's directions. I began to fear it would not work. And then it happened. All at once it was as if something in my mind had shifted—like changing glasses. In an instant I saw. Not simply with my eyes, because I still saw the stars, and yet somehow I did not. I was no longer lying on the earth; I was floating out in the infinite universe—though I had not fallen asleep. I was completely awake. I had never been so awake, so alive. And the universe revealed itself, and then it was there before me—no, it was everywhere. I cannot express with enough precision, in enough exact words, the magnificent feeling that took hold of me. My heart filled with a mixture of joy, gratitude, longing, awe, humility, and fear. It was unspeakably uplifting—the experience of recognizing your own insignificance, of feeling smaller than a speck of dust. And yet you know, with certainty, that you are part of the whole, and that the bond of belonging never loosens its grip, never leaves you. My soul soared. It wanted to go home into God. Meanwhile my body was terrified; it sensed what death is, because to enter the same dimension as God is not an experience meant for a physical body. It is dazzling—and it is terrible. It lasted only a few moments. The instant my being comprehended God, His vastness struck me down. I could not endure it. I sat up at once, then dropped to my knees, my hands clawing at the grass so I would not dissolve and cease to exist. There I was on my knees before God—though I had always believed I would never do such a thing, and that no one could ever make me. I had to realize: yes, no human being could ever make me. But God could.

For about fifteen minutes I could not stand, could not sit, could not lie down. Collapsed to my knees, my forehead pressed to the earth, I gathered every scrap of strength and gripped clumps of grass with both hands. I felt unworthy to lift my head. And even if I had tried, I could not have. I could not move. Eyes lowered, trembling in an ecstasy mixed with fear, I bowed beneath the weight of God pressing down on my shoulders. He fell over me like a vast blanket covering everything. I could barely breathe, and I felt incapable of receiving the immeasurable reality that had suddenly settled onto me. I felt His power, His weight. I was conscious that He is alive, and I bowed before His commanding greatness—which, despite everything, radiated encouragement, acceptance, and love. The realization paralyzed me for long minutes. After a while I became aware that my mentor was laughing at me. He knew what I would go through, and he took genuine amusement in it—me, who once was so in love with herself, now on the ground on her knees, forced to understand what nothing she truly is. Even recalling this experience floods me with indescribable euphoria and happiness. And yet I would not be able to do it again. Even though I could now do it alone. Until then I believed there was a God. From that moment on, I knew. That is true certainty. They can take from me anything that belongs to the material world—but not this. No one can. Because it is mine now. It lives in my soul. It burned itself into me forever. It does not let go—and I do not let go either. I am a tiny microparticle of the whole. Today I know my task is to fulfill the purposes for which I was born. The rest—only God knows.

I wish for every human being that they, too, like me, may become part of this experience while still alive.

A Cruise, Differently

Thirteen years after my Caribbean ordeal, another cruise awaited me—almost as if it were placing a frame around the life I had lived so far. My mentor honored me—and one other mentee as well, Emery—by taking us on a Mediterranean cruise for a week. He must have had a good reason, though he did not reveal it to us. In time, however, it became clear to me. This voyage, too, was "arranged" by my mentor, but it differed radically from the previous one. It was a heartwarming, deeply spiritual experience. If I had to compare it to anything, I would say it was as though I had stepped into an alternate reality— into a world that exists in parallel with the one we call real. I didn't know what to expect, because my earlier cruise adventure is still vivid in me.

What I lived through this time was the perfect opposite of my Caribbean journey—unforgettable, and soul-soothing at once.

We took a circuit on the Costa cruise line's ship called *Diadema*, stopping at Rome – Savona – Marseille – Barcelona – Palma de Mallorca – Cagliari – Rome. In my previous account I mentioned how enormous that ship had been. Well, this ship—despite my prior experience—was still shocking to me: at least twice the size of the other. With nearly forty yards of width and more than three hundred yards of length, it was, quite simply, gigantic. Because of that, every day brought several miles of walking—even without counting the city tours. The ship itself was beautiful, defined by an Italian design that suited our taste perfectly. A passenger load of four thousand nine hundred and fifty was served by a crew of twelve hundred and fifty, with the greatest devotion and care. Whatever problem or worry came up, they were unfailingly accommodating, doing everything they could to ensure every guest felt good. This ship also traveled at night and arrived in the next city's harbor by morning. Since we had balcony cabins—and I'm an early riser—I stepped out onto my balcony almost every morning to admire the sunrise and watch the docking. Usually, I would already find my mentor on his own balcony, because our cabins were next to each other. After the day's organized excursions—or our free wandering—around five or six in the late afternoon we would weigh anchor, and Andrea Bocelli's *Con Te Partirò*—or, as most people know it, *Time To Say Goodbye*—would send us off from the place we were leaving behind. To this day, whenever I hear that song, I become so overwhelmed that I always end up crying. We gathered unforgettable experiences everywhere—and not only because of the marvelous cities. The special, calming aura surrounding my mentor played its part as well. As I've already said, this cruise cannot be compared to my first Caribbean cruise, whose purpose was to test me. Through trials that pushed me to the edge, I fought almost for survival. This one, by contrast, felt like a reward for everything I had done and achieved so far. The whole journey was light, liberated, effortless.

From Rome, a private driver took us to the departure point, the harbor of a small town called Civitavecchia. The town showed us its sweetest face. I would gladly spend a few days there someday. After we stood marveling at the unbelievable size of our ship, we settled into our cabins and began exploring. I could hardly wait for departure. At five in the afternoon the moment arrived, and at last we sailed out to sea. My second voyage began—one that became, forever and indelibly, part of my soul. First stop: Savona. When we arrived the next day, it was magnificent—and also a little frightening—to watch this colossal ship maneuver into such a tiny harbor. Our ship was the largest "building" in the entire city, almost crushing its surroundings by sheer scale. Even the tourists walking along the waterfront stopped, astonished by the disproportion. Here we could already taste the Mediterranean mood, the feeling of life. We stood looking on dreamily as an old fisherman unhurriedly prepared his boat for the day. Our stroll continued through the fish market, where we saw countless sea creatures unfamiliar to us— yet clearly in high demand among the buyers. And the walk did not end there. As we wandered, we noticed how practical their architecture was— how perfectly it took the climate into account. In the narrow alleys between houses built tightly side by side, the air was so cool I nearly shivered each time we passed the mouth of one. Outside, the heat was almost unbearable, and suddenly we understood how the people who live here can endure it. Back on the ship we withdrew to our cabins, refreshed ourselves, and then talked through the day's events. Nothing "special" had happened—and yet a strange euphoria came over me. Somehow my mentor brought us into a way of sensing reality the way he does. For me it was an extraordinary, transcendent experience, one I can hardly even put into words. Later, at dinner, Emery received a small etiquette lesson as well—because no deficiency is so trivial that our Angel wouldn't address it. After that, only a pleasant, restful night remained.

New morning, new city. In Marseille we didn't want to follow the tourist flood, so we wandered like explorers through a less visited part of town—which, being Sunday, didn't show much of itself. It couldn't truly take hold of us. And yet this place is unforgettable to me for one particular reason. In the harbor, a line of vendors offered their tempting goods. And since we have a sweet tooth, what else could we buy but Marseille's characteristic treat—orange cookies. At that point I had had no sense of smell for ten years, the consequence of a botched nose surgery. They held different cookies under my nose—anise, orange, lavender—and I smelled nothing. We tasted them, and since they were supposedly delicious, we stocked up generously. When we returned to the ship after sightseeing, we went into my mentor's cabin and talked through what we'd experienced. The cookies came out. They were luxuriating in the cloud of fragrance, and I could only watch them. I regretted being left out. But I wasn't left out in the end. My mentor called me over and said, "All right. Come here. I'll fix your nose now." For anyone who doesn't know: losing your sense of smell is a serious problem. People joke, "Lucky you, you don't smell unpleasant things," but it stops being funny when you can't tell food has spoiled, when you can't smell smoke if the house catches fire. And when you can't taste properly—because smell is part of tasting—eating loses its pleasure. To me, the Marseille orange cookie felt like a sponge-cake-based biscuit. Since I couldn't smell it, it held nothing special. So I was genuinely happy that he offered to put my nose right. I had asked him many times, and he had always refused. He only does something if, in his judgment, it serves a truly useful purpose. I deliberately used the phrase *put it right* instead of *heal*. He rejects the idea that he "heals," because, as he says, he is not a healer and not a doctor. He works with the development of the soul—with what is eternal, not what is perishable. But if something is malfunctioning, he can correct it—whether it's a flawed character trait or a wound of the spirit born from trauma. Or even a personal error, a societal-level problem—he can correct that too, if asked. In my case, my nose wasn't working properly, so he "corrected" it. He did not "heal" it. Over time, I came to understand the difference.

He sat me down and placed his hand on my nose. It wasn't painful at all—more like warmth, a faint scraping sensation, a tingling. It felt as though every cell inside my nose had awakened and was searching for its place. It resembled the feeling of a leg falling asleep, and then life rushing back in. After a few minutes, when he stopped, he took one of the bags, handed it to me, and told me to smell it. I wanted to smell the cookies so badly that I inhaled deeply from the bag. In that instant, it was as if my nose exploded—an orange scent hit me with such brutal intensity. I jolted backward from the shock and the force of it and could only blurt out, "Ugh, this is horrible! Awful! It's so strong—like sniffing pure orange oil!" The room burst into laughter. In my joy I started smelling everything—the other cookies, the soap, the bedspread, my clothes, even my perfume, because I had never smelled that either. It had been chosen for me on faith—"Believe us, it suits you"—and it truly did. But it didn't end there. Emery, emboldened by this success, asked him whether he would fix his wrist, because for three weeks he'd been suffering from tendonitis and the pain wouldn't ease. He could barely use his hand; even lifting a bottle of water was difficult. Our mentor sat him down in front of him and held his wrist. After a few minutes, the pain was gone. He could lean on it, twist it, load it—no pain, and it never returned. Sadly, he still couldn't be persuaded to take on further "cases." He deflects requests by saying: if you're sick, go to a doctor. In his view, modern medicine and pharmacology should be valued more. He hopes medicine will soon reach a level where ancient and alternative healing methods will no longer be necessary. He encourages everyone to appreciate doctors more—morally and financially. He helped me because conventional medical tools could not have restored my sense of smell. In Emery's case, there were practical reasons related to the trip.

The next morning, the rising sun found us in Barcelona. I assumed it would be beautiful, filled with sights—Gaudí, for instance. I hardly need to list the reasons it's considered one of Europe's most distinctive tourist destinations. I wasn't disappointed. But it wasn't only the attractions—truly breathtaking—that made the city special for me. It was how livable it felt. Barcelona is not a display window. They take the needs and habits of residents and tourists into serious account.

There is greenery everywhere, and even more benches. Clean, wide streets and sidewalks. It gave me a sense of home, of friendliness. I knew immediately: it must be good to live here. We didn't have much time, so we chose a sightseeing bus to cover more ground and gather a stronger impression. It was a good decision: in a short time we received far more—and deeper—impact than we would have wandering on foot until our strength ran out. The bus's starting and ending point was Ciutadella Park. Our first destination, like proper tourists, was the Sagrada Família. Needless to say, an immense crowd was trying to get inside. We had planned the same, but the prospect of waiting for hours killed the idea, so we admired it only from the outside. We fled the heat into the park across the street, where a swarm of souvenir vendors awaited tourists—which we, of course, did not skip. In that park we found an ice-cream seller offering the best, most delicious ice cream of the entire trip. We still talk about it. Because we managed our time and energy well, we returned to the ship at day's end not exhausted, but happily filled with the day's pleasures. When Bocelli's song rose at departure, it softened all of us, and we knew we would return here one day. Of course, even this day did not end without something extraordinary. That night my mentor had one more surprise—another proof of his peculiar way of seeing. Long after dinner he told us to get ready, because we were going up to the top of the ship: he wanted to show us something. After no small amount of elevators and stairs, we reached the top. Up there, there was barely any light. He told us to go to the darkest part, all the way to the railing. We did. Then he asked us to close our eyes for a minute, and when we opened them, to look far out across the sea. I closed my eyes. When I opened them, my breath caught. About a mile away from our ship, another massive cruise liner hovered on the water, fully illuminated. It looked as though it were floating in outer space, because you couldn't tell where the sky began and where the perfectly smooth sea began—the sea reflecting the stars. It was an incredible sight, an unbelievable experience.

A short, restful night—and then the long-awaited Palma de Mallorca: the paradise of sea and swimming. If you spend time with an Angel, you'd better be prepared: nothing happens with him the way you would expect. Naturally, that was true now as well. The moment we docked, nearly all passengers poured off the ship at once and attacked the nearest beach. I don't need to describe what that must have looked like. So came another solution typical of my mentor. He said we should find a taxi to take us to the best beach on the island. All right—another beach, then. But of course that wasn't the point. Emery and I found a very cheerful driver who—for not a small sum—drove us to the far side of the island. My mentor didn't care about the cost, because naturally there was a hidden purpose even in this choice. We drove for more than an hour, cutting across the "real" Mallorca—not as glossy, not as tourist-friendly, and yet worth it. For more than one reason. The beach lay in a gorgeous cove: water blue as a fairy tale, white sand, and no crowds. The experience was crowned by what we discovered when we ate lunch at the restaurant of the hotel there. He made us understand: never stare at the glittering splendor in front; look at what is behind things in truth. Because of that, even in something as simple as seeing Mallorca's real face, we learned that you can only form an objective picture of a society, a place, if you also see the "backyard." After lunch we rested a while longer, then called the taxi and returned to our ship. Another strange and wonderful day.

On the last day, on the island of Sardinia, we visited Cagliari. A charming little city, but because of the intense heat we didn't linger long;

we spent most of the rest of the day on the ship. This day belonged to rest. We had many programs to choose from, and we tried quite a few—or simply enjoyed the shows. We saw dolphins swimming alongside our ship, or stretched out on deck loungers and took in the seemingly endless sea. Meanwhile I tried to capture, as deeply as possible, and lock into my heart, the effect that this revealed spiritual world had on my soul throughout this miraculous journey.

I returned home with unforgettable memories and a wealth of experience, because this "vacation" was not travel for its own sake, but an exercise as well. My mentor, day by day, with a multitude of small tasks, welded Emery and me together. The two of us had found cooperation difficult before—but this trip changed our relationship at its foundation. Since then, our bond has strengthened in an incredible way. We can always rely on one another. That is when it became clear what the purpose of this journey truly was, beyond rest and pleasure. First: learning and growth. Second: it is extremely important to my mentor that those for whom he takes responsibility—and with whom he works, often for decades—also live in harmony with one another. Because whoever walks the path he offers doesn't only receive from it; they must also do their part. And that can only be achieved through harmonious cooperation. In that sense, Emery and I were weak links. And yet, on this trip, my mentor made our relationship turn one hundred and eighty degrees. And I will say it: that is no small achievement.

The most important years of my life lie between the Caribbean cruise and the Mediterranean cruise. Compared to the first, the second differed in this: the first was an outer journey, where I had to face trials. The second was an inner voyage. It wasn't special because of unbelievable adventures, but because of an unfathomable Soul—and the kind of lived experience that becomes possible through him. That is why it is so hard for me to write about this journey. It was so intimate, so soul-caressing, that words can't hold it. Perhaps a poet could give back the feeling I carried throughout, because its spiritual effect is so different from anything ordinary, anything reachable. On both cruises I watched sunrises, and yet the difference between them was beyond comparison. You cannot describe what it means to hear the sea's low thunder, to watch gulls in flight, to see the rising sun, or to watch a pillar of sunlight sink deep into the water—when you are seeing it together with an Angel. How can I explain what mark all this left in my soul? This journey was carefree and bright, rich with experiences that could only have been what they were because of his presence. Simply being near him is a meditative state. Living events with him is not an everyday thing. Through him, places and moments become experiences of the spirit. Experiences such that, whenever you think of them again, the intimate calm of a happy home and a warm, joyful contentment washes through you. If I could, I would share with everyone the feeling that rises in me whenever I recall those days. And I wish, dear Reader, that one day you too may take part in such an inner voyage. Who knows—perhaps one day we will travel on the same ship.

In Closing

With rare exceptions, people don't really like to think. I was the same. As a child they even used to tell me, "Hilda, don't think—just do what I tell you!" So after a while I stopped. Later it started to feel tiring. More than that—I got frightened of my own thoughts, so I kept myself busy even when I didn't have to. I "occupied" myself, just so I wouldn't have to face myself. And yet there were many stretches of my life when no distraction existed that could chase off my tormenting thoughts. Then I was forced to stop and think—about my life, my missed chances, my wrong turns. It was beside my mentor that I learned to think again, to use my mind. I remember how many times, before him, I woke in the middle of the night because a problem wouldn't let me rest—and every time I brushed it away with the thought that night is for sleeping, not for overthinking. He opened my eyes to what a mistake that was. Today, for instance, I know that if I wake between two and four in the morning, there's a serious reason for it, and I will think through the problem that surfaced until I solve it. If I have to, I won't close my eyes again until morning. But in that open state of mind, a solution usually comes quickly. Then I can fall back asleep and sink into a restful, healing kind of dream. I can only encourage everyone to listen to the signals of their mind— and no matter what time of day it is, to think about the problem that arises. The same is true of self-knowledge. Now I am willing to face my flaws and bad decisions on any day of the year. I think through what I did well and what I did poorly—and why. In this way, the days of facing myself aren't about guilt, self-flagellation, or self-pity, but about living life with joy. Life is a thing that includes mistakes. Not on purpose, not deliberately—but we do make them. Our spiritual stature is shown by how capable we are of seeing those mistakes in ourselves. When judging others, our critical sense works beautifully. But our own portrait—we go on seeing it as lovely and spotless for a very long time. Through great determination and an immense amount of work, I became able to see my true face in the mirror. That is what set the change in motion—the change that made a new person look back at me. And when that happened, I saw behind the face my own wonderful, pure-hearted child-self, forgotten somewhere deep down, who had wanted to break free—and who was finally given a chance. I learned that life is the greatest grace I could have been given. And my life includes the many trials through which I can prove I deserve to move forward. I learned that I don't have to be afraid of anyone—and that there are proper tools for solving problems; I simply have to become capable of finding them and using them. I had to learn how to make the most of the tools available to me so that I could prevail without having to crush anyone in the process. I had to learn that I must not run from conflicts, but work through them—and that there is no lost cause, because you cannot, and must not, give up. And it is also important to understand that "you must never give up" is not the same as charging into the wall a hundred times without thinking. When I want to reach a goal, I try. If there is a path that turns out not to lead there because it's a dead end, then I change direction at once—flexibly—and look for a new route. And I must keep doing that until I reach the goal, otherwise I fail. A human being is not here to lose. That is how I make myself fit to step to a higher level.

I wouldn't trade my life with anyone's. I would do nothing differently than what I have done over the past decades. Today I am truly happy. I am unspeakably grateful to God—and to the Angel who led me to Him, my mentor—that I can be where I am, and as I am. With every action I try to repay the opportunity I was given. And as a sign of my gratitude, the least I can do is pass on the knowledge and experience I received to others who need it. I am not saying by this that I already know everything. I am very far from that—but that isn't the point. All my life, I too waited for a sign that would make me brave enough to step out of the mistaken life I had been living. But no matter how many signs I received, I kept making excuses—why not now, why I couldn't, why I mustn't. All I can say to everyone is that it is never too late to begin. Because even the one who reaches the point of beginning has already taken the first step—by arriving at the threshold where they can begin. My intention with this writing was to share with others the positive way of relating to life that now defines me; the radical change in my worldview; the rebirth and growth of my self-respect—everything that made me happy and balanced. With everyone who needs it and wants it. I wish that everyone finds harmony in their life, and if this writing helped even one single person do that, then I am happy. As a final word, I would give people only one piece of advice. No matter how their lives unfold, let them always remember: as long as there is a next day, there is a chance! And to close, a quotation from my wonderful mentor—a true Angel—which, to me, captures the change I have lived through:

"Your wisdom is the knowledge and understanding that arise from correctly evaluating and integrating the experiences shaped by the life events, influences, and trials you have faced—and which you then instinctively draw upon when making the right decisions in the trial of your life."

My Angel mentor and I at the beginning of our acquaintance

With the kind and very friendly captain of my first cruise

An adventure park in Cancun – the turning point of my Caribbean journey

Surrounded by my selfless and dear Italian friends during my Caribbean cruise

With Angelo, a true friend of mine, the savior sent by my mentor

Dwarfed by the impressive size of the ship on our second cruise

After the ice cream (with our Angel mentor and Emery)

Walking the streets of Cagliari

My mentor and I 22 years after we met

I am my own master